KEN WHITEHEAD'S
PIKE FISHING

KEN WHITEHEAD'S PIKE FISHING

Ken Whitehead

David & Charles
Newton Abbot London North Pomfret (Vt)

The book is dedicated to all pike anglers
who measure their success in pleasure,
and not pure pounds and ounces

British Library Cataloguing in Publication Data

Whitehead, Ken, *1930 Aug. 10–*
   Ken Whitehead's pike fishing.
   1. Pike fishing
   I. Title
   799.1′753   SH691.P6
   ISBN 0–7153–8920–3

Phototypeset by Northern Phototypesetting Co, Bolton
and printed in Great Britain
by Redwood Burn Ltd, Trowbridge
for David & Charles Publishers plc
Brunel House Newton Abbot Devon

Published in the United States of America
by David & Charles Inc
North Pomfret Vermont 05053 USA

Preface

There should always be a very good reason for writing a book of any kind. Some are written for their technical value, others to celebrate great events, strange happenings, or as a record of the past. In this book I have tried to include a little of each of these things.

It has been my privilege to have been a pike fisherman for nearly as long as I can remember and during that time I have enjoyed both memorable and disastrous days' sport in every type of imaginable surroundings. Better still, I have experienced the joys of fishing with others whose humour and skills have been second to none.

Through the pages that follow I have set out just a few of the happenings that have come readily to mind: over 50 years of sport there have been a host of other incidents, some similar, some even more outrageous than the ones I have described, that surface occasionally, then sink like a punctured float to defy recall.

I have deliberately avoided a mass of tackle details, such as test curves, breaking strains and other 'scientific' facts. There is on the market already a multitude of books dealing with these details, instead, I have concentrated on that which concerns the actual attraction and taking of pike by methods that by long trial and error I have come to adopt as my standards. Especially I have included my failures and some possible reasons for them, knowing that no angler will ever achieve perfection – not until he meets the Big Fisherman.

As to the future – well, most anglers shrug and indicate that the future of pike fishing is anyone's guess. But it is not, for the future is firmly our own to command. In the final chapter I have tried to evaluate how far we have come and where we could, and possibly should, aim. Many will disagree, but we cannot bandy worlds for ever. Sooner or later we must unite with definite aims that will improve not only the image of pike, but that of the pike angler as well.

I would like to give grateful thanks to Barrie Rickards not only for the Foreword he has written to this book and for the many years of happy, easy-going friendship we have shared, but also for the diagrams that appear here. Vic Gibson must also be mentioned – no one can wind me up into think-mode more quickly than half an hour's conversation with this outstanding pikeman – and, not least, Len Cacutt not only for his editing of my manuscript but for the encouragement and understanding he has shown in dealing with any problems that have arisen.

Ken Whitehead
HAILSHAM, EAST SUSSEX

Contents

Foreword

You'll enjoy this book! Ken Whitehead is one of those awkward so-and-so's who thinks instead of copying. I've known him many years now and, indeed, we have co-authored quite a few books. Although he follows the very serious literature in books, he tends only irregularly to scan the weekly angling newspapers and monthly glossies. This means that he is always slightly out of phase with the latest angling fad and fetish. But it means that when he makes a statement it is influenced only by his own experience and that of his closest colleagues, with whom he often discusses problems. His tackle, techniques and philosophies are shaped by the same ruthless chisel: slavishly following others is one thing, fashioning your own destiny, even in a small way, is quite another. It leads to mistakes but it also leads to discoveries, and to the thorough testing of everything to do with your fishing.

Ken Whitehead's testing began as a youngster almost 50 years ago on the Pevensey Marshes – he was one of the first drain addicts, if you will! He has also done a lot of river piking, one of the few to do so on the Thames and elsewhere. And it is of interest to me that with all the variety of piking he has done, including varied stillwaters, he uses a relatively small range of rigs. I am the same; in my opinion, a good, home-made snap tackle covers most circumstances quite well. However, whereas I tend to use a float for paternoster work, Ken sticks the rod up in the air to put the bait in exactly the right position with respect to the bottom. All these things he has worked out from first principles. What I especially like is that he rejects the fancy and the complicated. There is far too much of that in modern piking and it is largely unnecessary.

So, too, I find an affinity with his thoughts on pike distribution – hotspots and holding areas – and also with his appreciation of the role and influence of the weather conditions. Like myself he probably fishes anyway, whatever the elements produce, and that in itself leads one to amass enough experience to make judgements. But above all, Ken's book is a personal record not only of his progress but of his enjoyments, his likes and his dislikes. Throughout the text there are a number of salutary lessons for us all, and these are particularly crystallised in the final chapter – the Future.

It is the work and thinking of experienced anglers like Ken Whitehead that both records our angling past and plots our angling future. Even when we find ourselves disagreeing with detail, or a particular argument, we should read carefully, note, and store it for the future. I happen to believe that the public – or, rather, the Lefties – will soon turn against anyone who eats anything that is not vegetable. That time is almost on us. I have met people who are extremely rude, to my face, about my liking for cooked fish, fowl and some red meat. They just cannot contemplate another's viewpoint. Ken Whitehead, in his final synthesis, does offer an alternative scenario for some of today's pikers. They would be wise to accept that offer if they have any thought at all for the future. The trout reservoir managers would also fare well if they heeded Ken's advice – there again his own experiences coincide exactly with my own – and we have never even discussed the subject in spite of our long association.

Here, then, is one man's piking, beautifully steeped in the old days, which he describes with a good eye, not wholly with nostalgia, and then leads through to the present, culminating with a stab at the future. If there is one appeal, one message, in this book it is that the pike angler, while enjoying himself, must proceed with commonsense and an understanding of proportion – fanaticism in almost any form is out.

Barrie Rickards
MILTON, CAMBRIDGE

1
Early Beginnings

A piercing north-east wind drives powder-fine snowflakes through the night outside, coating and covering every surface, invading and filling each tiny chink and crevice with a white, crisp blanket. Below the house, where the flat and wide expanse of Sussex's Pevensey Marshes allows the full fury of the gale spawned on the steppes of Siberia to shriek uninterrupted, settled snow has filled every frozen gut and killick until not a drainage channel of any sort is visible. Yet that self-same glacial wind of terror brings with it Pink Foot and White Front geese to mix with Brent, Canada and huge Bewick swans all of which yelp, bark and cry in a chorus that rises above the blizzard's roar. In contrast, the silence of the room is broken only by the crackle and hiss from burning apple logs and the gentle snores from the labrador, dreaming no doubt of endless hedges and running, twisting rabbits.

Around the room lies a tangle of rods and reels, lures, floats and nets together with tackle bags, bait tins and, in the fireplace a pair of waders drying out and awaiting that final checkover before being packed ready for the next outing.

The weather had been well-forecast. After climbing gates and side-stepping across plank-wide footbridges that are the only highways across the marshland, I watched thin, dawn-red sunlight barely touch the land before being swallowed by lowering clouds that pushed an oppressive silence from horizon to horizon, warning everyone that Nature would seek retribution for the open weather that had lasted for nigh-on a fortnight. There was an uneasiness, an awareness of trials to come, that caused wildlife to stir and move and my hopes were that pike lying among the network of waterways would be touched with that same unrest and feed against the closing weather.

Marshland fishing is never easy: water levels change constantly, the

1 Flat, open, exposed to wind and rain, the marsh offers no cover or shelter. It is no place to fish unless the angler studies detail, waits, and – most importantly – keeps out of sight. Plank-wide footbridges are the only ways across these bleak places

smallness of dykes and ditches and a lack of shade and cover, other than during summer months when weedgrowth all but chokes a bait as it enters the water, bring a formidable challenge. No two days are the same – and no two days' fishing styles will guarantee success for what scores on the one will remain unproductive on the other.

I had started on a 4m (15ft) gut – large by marshland standards – but which demanded long, accurate casting to place a bait where it would enjoy some chance of success. The pattern of dredging and marsh drainage presents an interesting parallel in that the usual V-shaped section soon alters through erosion and more especially deposition so that the centre of the V fills and weeds over to pack and lie until a W-section forms with deep channels practically under the banks' edge. Pike lie in those two parallel channels which permit deeper water and to find them demands that one casts anything up to 36·5m (40yd) up or down the gut, then gently draws the bait back towards the rod until it suddenly and silently enters an area of water completely undisturbed by angler or splash from a falling bait. Twenty minutes, perhaps half an hour later the bait is moved closer still until either a take occurs or the cast is exhausted, when it then becomes necessary to move and start again. The rod must have a sensitive tip section that can handle both line and bait with accuracy, even the lightest sprat, the most usual offering mounted on a single tail and treble gill hook. Sometimes the float must be the smallest of pilots. Often, when the water is that gin-clear colour that follows continued nights of frost and windless days, it is an unpainted bottle cork that is used to record the position of the bait so that you retain some idea of where each cast has reached, preventing unnecessary over-casting in a particular area.

Few pikemen really fish the marshes, the small size of many of the waterways perhaps convinces them that good fish could not lie in water only 1m (3ft) deep in ditches some 1·2m (4ft) wide. Even those who acknowledge the existence of pike there prefer large lakes and rivers where casts necessitating brute force to cover long distances are considered more likely to find a fish than the hands-and-knees crawl, the deadly accurate cast which must be made from a sitting or squatting position, and the utter silence needed to convince pike that they are completely safe from attack.

It was three hours before I scored with a fish, during which time I experimented by using baits injected with air to lift them just off the bottom, to fully legered baits secured to the bed by groundbait cannisters that exuded fish oil. Eventually I hit on the taking formula for the day. It required a long cast together with an extra 0·6m (2ft) between bait and cork float, that allowed a swooping, tumbling action as the bait was cast and then retrieved slowly 30cm (1ft) or so at a time, using just three turns of the reel handle before a pause of a minute or so, then a repeat of that seductive retrieval once more.

The first fish took with a swirl and confidence that promised more in the way of weight than the 3·6kg (8lb) that finally registered on the scales. But there was ample compromise in the shape of the head, which was broad and distinguished without the usual narrow, brainless appearance which seems to dog small pike in general and even larger fish in some waters. The slight kype to its lower jaw was in keeping with the weight and did not give an appearance of age, while the facial marking was bold and even. I would rather have banked that fish than one of twice the weight but of indifferent appearance.

The second and only other fish of the day was a twice-taker for which greed produced a downfall. On the marshes it is unusual to encounter the widespread dropped-bait syndrome that is being forced onto our other waters by sheer over-fishing, and when I felt the slight tug, a mere hold while retrieving, then felt the line pull free, I knew it was only by accident and not suspicion that I had lost the fish. Twenty minutes later a fresh cast working the sprat over the same position produced a boisterous jagging fight from a fish that tail-walked once for a metre or so then settled into some debris accumulated on the centre ridge of the channel. A slow walk above the fish and some gentle pressure brought it back into play and eventually onto the bank where it showed that its 4kg (9lb)-plus was largely stored in broad, muscular shoulders that had helped provide its strength during the fight. Altogether it was a typical marshland pike outing, one of a hundred similar days of enjoyment, measured not in weight of fish but in pleasure and relaxation. But there had been many other days in the past when far more fish were taken, often not all by legal means, nor even means that would be remotely acceptable by today's fishing standards. The Depression of the 1930s produced men hardened by hunger and driven by desperation to fish for food, for whom the niceties of sportsmanship meant very little.

Archie Marchant was a giant and hero to the small boy of eight years who lived, ate and slept fishing. The man's size was relative to that of a lad who, in village terminology, stood just 'two hands' high. But the enormous bush of white hair and mutton-chop whiskers that framed high cheekbones tanned by the weather until they were a matching brown to the boots, gaiters and corduroy trousers, made the figure a man never to be forgotten. As a marshman Archie had no rival. He had spent years digging out drains and ditches, a rheumatic and back-breaking occupation that disappeared with the advent of the mechanical digger, leaving him to support a wife and two terrier dogs largely by his wits. I was discovered by Archie on an early autumn day fishing for pike on a drain that I felt to be safe from prying eyes but, to someone who could sight a hare lying against a dead background at 90m (100yd) as obvious as the monstrous pike float that always accompanied me whether fishing or not.

I had been smitten by 'pikeitis' two years earlier on the first occasion that I saw a man fishing. He stood at the side of the Kennet and Avon Canal and had two rods propped in front of the water, to one of which was attached a slender quill that stood motionless. To the line from the other rod was fastened a round, fat float that bobbed and swayed, sending thin ripples across the water to break the cloud and tree reflections on the surface. Badgering him for information I learned that the movement came from a small fish tethered below the surface and intended for a much bigger fish called a pike, which if his story was to be believed, was quite capable of jumping out of the water onto the bank and devouring both rod and fisherman before disappearing back into the depths.

From there it was but a short step to the acquisition of Bickerdyke's *Angling for Pike* and this completed the incubation period of my 'pikeitis'. This book ravished my imagination and filled my mind with pictures of great treble hooks, steel traces, huge-hooked gaffs, enormous wooden rods and, above all, the round floats that were the means of communication between man and pike. To Bickerdyke's everlasting glory even now I have only to pick up my worn, torn edition of his book to recapture the flood of anticipation, that flutter of the stomach that comes to those who can consider nothing greater in life than fishing for pike.

So it was that Archie found me sitting behind a bamboo garden-cane about 2·5m (8ft) long, around one end of which was wound a length of carpet thread. At the other end of the thread was a roughly carved circle of cork pierced with a porcupine quill, largely painted red. Below that hung a jaded roach trying to break free from a Jardine snap tackle that was strong enough to hold open the sluice gates that lay a mile or so downstream. Archie expressed no surprise at my being on what was private land, and passed no comment at the coarseness of my equipment. Instead, he sat down and talked fish and fishing for upwards of two hours, during which time I discovered how little I knew about the subject. He learned that I had not seen a pike in the flesh, so to speak, and when he invited me to go with him to catch a pike or two during the following week I nearly passed out with excitement.

We met on a still morning of light frost and marshland mist that almost hid Archie from view. In fact, had it not been for the enormous pole that he carried rather in the manner of a shepherd's crook I might have missed him altogether. Over one shoulder was a large canvas bag and his free hand held a livebait kettle that sloshed water over the lid with every step taken along the bank. Few words were exchanged as we plodded along a small gut that, compared with its neighbours, was relatively weed free.

Without warning the pole was lowered to the ground and the bag flung down beside it. Once the livebait can was settled safely, Archie began to put together some fishing tackle the likes of which I had never seen before – and only once since. From the bag came a dozen round pieces of wood about the size of a dinner-plate, each of which was painted green on one side and red on the other. Through the centre ran a hole and this was plugged first with a length of cord, then a piece of dowling that made a tight push-fit. One end of the cord was then tied round the dowling while the longer, remaining end was led carefully over the green side of the wooden circle before being attached to a large, murderous snap tackle formed of rusty hooks with hawser-strength gimp.

The livebait can provided a lively roach to be mounted onto the tackle and then the whole thing was balanced over the end of the pole, held out over the water towards midstream and gently lowered so that it floated, green-side up, the cord leading into the depths and the livebait tethered below. This piece of equipment, Archie informed me, was a trimmer and though he did not say that it was also a highly illegal and particularly killing method of poaching, I sensed that it was not entirely above-board by the constant sweeping glances he directed around the flat, open horizon.

With a dozen trimmers set out at intervals along the 366m (400yd) length of water, we sat down and waited for results. In front of us, each disc gyrated and bobbed as the fish below tried to free itself, unwittingly making a perfect target for any pike in the vicinity. As we

2 The trimmer is an age-old, all-killing method of piking much favoured by poachers. The livebait is tethered below the wooden disc and once the fish has been swallowed the disc flips over to show the take, and follows the pike until it is exhausted and can be pulled ashore

watched and waited, Archie explained that once a pike took hold of the bait it was as good as dead, because the trimmer would not only mark its position on the water but also play it until the fish was exhausted and unable to swim away. As we talked, one green circle began to bob, then suddenly flipped over until the red side lay on the surface before bobbing below, to resurface again in a series of swoops, plunges and sharp dives. Archie made no attempt to retrieve the outfit, solemnly declaring that there was plenty of time before 'them 'ooks was in the pike's guts'. So we sat and Archie talked marshland talk about rich men who bought and sold land for cash on the slap of a hand; of poaching by poor men with longnets and dogs, whose hares and rabbits were sold by the sixpence (2½p). From that memorable day one tale still stands above all others, a description of a lake near Battle Abbey, Sussex, which Archie visited with a distant relative during World War I and where they practised the art of 'Huxing'. This was a means of catching pike with spinners tied by a length of line to the legs of domestic geese which were driven into swimming across the lake. Archie witnessed many a cruel struggle using this practice where on numerous occasions the towed spinners attracted and hooked a pike that immediately joined battle with the goose in a series of wing-beating, water-erupting clashes that led sometimes to the goose being dragged below the water and drowned. Mostly, though, the goose won and drew the exhausted pike to the bank.

Eventually, the long pole was lifted and we tramped along the bank to where the trimmer lay red-side up on the surface, no more than 2m (6ft) out, and Archie slipped the hooked end under the wooden platform, catching the line hanging below. Hand over hand, he drew the tackle to the bank, then threw the pole down, lay and reached out to grasp the line before drawing it – with the pike – onto the bank. The fish flapped several times, then stretched still.

It was the first pike I had ever seen and I knelt beside it, inspecting every scale, the hard, antagonistic stare from the yellow eyes, and the mottled green, gold and white colours, fascinated yet frightened of the needle-sharp teeth visible each time the flattened jaws involuntarily opened and closed. Archie worked steadily away, drawing trimmers ashore, some with pike attached, others just as they had been set but with exhausted and near-dead roach still attached. When all were secured, the line holding the trimmers was cut. Leaving the hooks embedded within the pike, each monstrous – so they seemed to me – fish was dropped into a sack, the tackles collapsed and stowed back in the canvas bag and we were away, walking back along the marshland road. Though I cannot remember the number of fish landed, I recall the satisfaction Archie expressed when he told me that there was a customer for each fish at a 'tanner (2½p) a go', an insignificant sum by today's standards but a fortune to a man with but 10 shillings (50p) a week of public money to exist on.

Not all was cruelty and poaching in the thirties. There was a fishing tackle shop in Eastbourne, Sussex, where most of my Saturday mornings were spent watching the windows full of tackle. Naturally, the biggest display featured sea-fishing tackle, with a short, thick greenheart pier-fishing rod that wouldn't have flexed even if hooked to the 'Queen Mary'; large whole-cane beachcasters that needed massive wooden Nottingham and Scarborough reels to hold the heavy plaited silk and cuttyhunk lines deemed necessary to control even the most modest-sized flatfish.

Because trout fishing in that part of East Sussex was confined to few

3 *The Hardy Silex reel, a Rolls Royce item of fishing tackle in its day, made to exacting tolerances. It had ball-bearing races and a slip brake. This reel was the yardstick for long casting before the introduction of cheap, mass-produced fixed-spool reels*

waters there was a great deal of coarse fishing tackle available, dwarfing the split-cane trout gear. But of pike fishing tackle, articles actually manufactured to deal with pike, there was very little. Occasionally there would be a short rod with a 'pike' label on it, whole cane butt and middle joint, massive brass ferrules, with a lancewood tip joint nearly as strong as those used in beachcasting, and boasting porcelain rod rings and push-winch fittings. Once there was a Hardy Silex reel (Photograph 3) which occupied pride of place, advertised as 'Essential for pike spinning': on one never-to-be-forgotten occasion I was admitted to the inner sanctum behind the counter and had a demonstration of the Malloch reel. The principle of the revolving drum was that it could be turned edgeways-on, allowing line to be pulled over the rim. It seemed as revolutionary as a present-day Jumbo jet compared with a Spitfire. But the reel remained unsold for weeks on end, perhaps because the price of £3 was more than one week's wages and probably because nobody trusted something new-fangled and different from that which any other angler was using.

More important to most who pike-fished was terminal tackle, the attachments that fitted to the polished and greased silk line, never below 4·5kg (10lb) breaking strain and often 7kg (15lb) and more. Floats (Photograph 4) were huge, varying from the old *Fishing Gazette* type with slit side and wooden plugs that invariably slipped at some time during the session, allowing the bait to go in one direction and the float body in another, to the more favoured and reliable quill and cork-bodied bung held by float-ring and wire end-eye. And of course there was the pilot float without which no self-respecting angler was seen, ostensibly to show the direction in which line was running once the float had disappeared, but in reality to provide one more object of fascination that could be watched for signs of a taking fish.

In a glass case beside the counter was set out the ironmongery of the day. Clumsy Jardine snap-tackles, gorge tackles of trebles with moulded lead weight set around the shank of the treble, everything streamlined to ease its passage down a pike's throat and into the stomach: Archer flights: Sprat spinners and Crocodile mounts. The latter monstrosities with enormous body clasps, spike, vanes and trebles would have been equally at home in a castle's torture chamber, but nobody ever questioned the aesthetic quality of the tackle. Of far greater importance was the fact that it was cheap and could be used repeatedly when mounted with a deadbait.

Money − it was the be-all and end-all governing the angler's performance and ultimately the results he produced. Few would bother to spin with copper or silver spoons, Colorado or Kidney spinners costing up to three shillings (15p) when they could be lost in minutes, or even contemplate the vast sum of £5 for one of Hardys' Elarex reels that would have eased once and for all the headache of casting straight from one of the wooden, walnut-turned Nottingham reels in general use.

Of course, there were those who in some small way tried to buck the system, one of whom was Harold Kitchener Randall, our village plumber, handyman and pike-fishing fanatic. He designed, manufactured and assembled his own fixed-spool reel that was as attractive as an empty fire grate (something it closely resembled, by weight at least) and as reliable as a three-speed watch. Even now I recall the vague principles, based on the Alcock-Stanley reel, that required the line to be lifted on and off a reciprocal spindle the size and shape of a crochet needle when casting or retrieving. Most of the pieces, including the ball-bearing bodywork, came from Meccano parts and turned brass fittings that either flew off at intervals or, worse, spun out of control, removing large pieces of skin from fingers and hands as they went.

But by and large the idea worked, as did the many rods and other accessories made at home and paraded on local waters, with emphasis on the word 'local.' Money, or rather the lack of it, precluded travel over greater distances than could be covered by the humble pedal cycle. Most villages had their ponds and lakes that boasted big pike. Whether they were actually present or not was of no great consequence because it was the boasting that mattered. It kept one trying, eternally hopeful that on one magic day a monster of some sort would turn up. In reality, any pike over 4·5kg (10lb) was deemed a monster in those days and the majority of fish taken from rivers at least were jacks in the region of 2·3kg (5lb) or so. Bigger fish were invariably taken from regions too many miles away to be reached by pushbike, but always the facts about size, fight put up and tackle needed to land the fish were known and handed on by word of mouth rather like folk tales.

I often wish I could have compared one of those spoken tenth-hand-or-so encounters with the actual event on the bank when the fish was taken, but fortunately the chance never came. Had it done so much of the early magic of pike fishing would have disappeared.

The first pike I saw taken by fair means, or nearly so, was caught, like the majority in those days, on ordinary coarse float-fishing tackle. It was on the Cuckmere river at the pool below Shermans Bridge over which Morris Eights and Austin Sevens rocketed at 40mph. Below the supports and through the pool the flow was a sedate 2mph or so and at the wide margins nothing rocked the flat lilypads which acted as landing strips for dragon and damsel flies. At the head of the pool the stranger had been fishing for several hours with small bream and roach to show for his labour during that day of warm autumn sun.

We watched as he landed another small roach and carefully unhooked it, placing it in his landing net and setting it in the water to keep the fish alive. Then he slowly untied the gut cast from the line, slid off the goose-quill float and in its place set up pilot and pike float, following that with a gimp-mounted Jardine snap-tackle. A foldover lead was attached, the live roach retrieved from the net and held squirming as the hooks were mounted in place.

Just to watch the bend in the tip of that old greenheart roach rod as the livebait was cast out was a joy to us boys who sat in a semi-circle

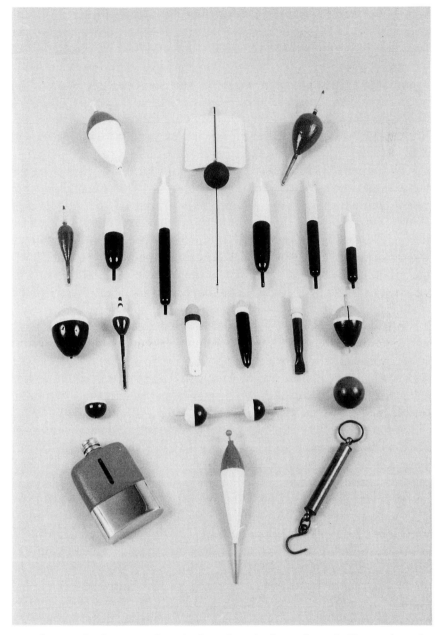

4 *Floats, which are nearly as bad as plugs for being hoarded by anglers; the author has yet to learn of any float being thrown away by an angler. The floats shown here belong to the author's collection, the flask and the spring balance being included to give an idea of scale*

behind the angler, fascinated as the line shot out and the bait hit the water under the bridge with a plop. For a moment it was still, then the float began to gyrate and slide slowly this way and that as the roach worked in the water. Ten minutes, an eternity, passed then suddenly some large unseen power beneath the surface took hold of the float and it slid silently and quickly into the depths, leaving the tiny red pilot float to tail across the surface, marking the position of the fish below. We waited, holding our breath, but the angler made no movement other than to strip some line free from the reel.

Although it is difficult without hindsight to estimate how long the fish was allowed to hold the bait before some loose line was reeled in it was at least another five minutes before the strike was delivered with a slow, steady sideways move. Other than a savage downward tug on the rod tip, nothing happened, then the reel clicked as line was pulled free and the fish was played. It was nothing spectacular – after all, a jack of 2·2kg (5lb) or so has limited strength even when played on fine tackle – but we stood, almost cheering, as the fish was brought to the net.

Once on the bank the line was cut, leaving the hooks set well down in the stomach and with a nod we were informed that the prize was ours if we wanted it. We did and I won the toss to keep the carcass which was carried home as if caught by myself, and eaten by the family. In those days it was the right thing to do and was the fate of almost every pike caught.

Then came the war and everything changed. The slow, steady pace of life disappeared with mechanization and mobilization. Rivers became training grounds, the south coast a battleground to be set with minefields and barbed wire that shut away hundreds of acres including prime fishing places. But worst of all was the sheer wantonness of it all.

One hot summer's day during the Battle of Britain we fished Shermans Bridge pool, one eye on the float, the other on the sky above. Nothing moved except white, smoky con-trails, reflected on the surface of the water. Suddenly a Bren-gun carrier pulled to a halt on the bridge and three soldiers appeared to watch our floats, jeering at our having caught nothing. We were used to it – fishing in those days of strain was something which attracted attention from Servicemen everywhere and we gave the usual excuses for our motionless floats. Then one of the soldiers spoke quietly to one of the others and told us to get well back from the water. We obeyed and watched in silence as a small Mills Bomb was pulled from a webbing pouch. Pulling the pin from the grenade the soldier threw it into the water and we flung ourselves to the ground.

It was a relatively small explosion and we walked forward to watch the water cease its bubbling and boiling. For a time, the muddy brown colour hid everything. Then, slowly, white bellies of fish rose and floated, first in twos and threes, eventually in dozens. Silently we watched an enormous shoal of bream wallow dead on the surface, bolstered by roach, perch, tench and three pike, the biggest considerably heavier than we had seen caught a year or so earlier.

Laughing, the soldiers invited us to pull the fish out and help ourselves, insisting that their style of 'fishing' was the only sensible one. We stood, silent and unmoving, until they roared up the road in their carrier. Finally giving up trying to find out how many fish had actually been killed we took down our now-useless fishing rods and walked home. As we went we decided that what we had seen wasn't fishing – it was sheer bloody murder.

When hostilities ceased then pike fishing was worse and not better. Those areas that had been shut off by the authorities and where we hoped to find virgin fishing were found to be polluted or, worse, cleared out by explosives. Many places were unapproachable for months – sometimes years – after the war because of uncleared mines and unexploded ammunition. And when the closed areas did come back into circulation there was little or no fishing tackle available for use other than that on the secondhand market. Tackle manufacturers were slow to convert from producing wartime wares to their prewar task of making rods, reels and lines so that the few items which did arrive in the shops were snapped up at prices way above those that could be afforded by the mass of anglers. The black market that arose in the used rod and reel market was unbelievable, prices sometimes reaching into the tens of pounds, costs unheard of even for brand new tackle a mere five years previously.

To complicate matters further travel was a nightmare. No petrol, no mass-produced cars or motorbikes – one could only pushbike and remain in the reasonable vicinity of one's home or use the railways – and they were in a sad and sorry state. Fortunately the workman's ticket that allowed cheap travel around the cities before 8am was available and this encouraged journeys from London (where I had moved to) to places as far as Reading and even beyond.

But for the masses it was stick to the waters around home and I was amazed to find pike in places I had never considered before. One of the best and most central in London was the lake in Battersea Park. Once through the gates, past where the barrage balloon was once moored beside the river, a large section was opened to anglers who fished for roach, bream, small perch and some sizeable but very wary carp.

I found myself part of a cut-throat crew devoted to all-out fishing in any form, comprising Bob, who was a crack steam-engine driver, often taking the Golden Arrow down to Dover twice a week; Harry, who was as Cockney a character as is possible to meet but who spoke with an impeccable Italian accent when working at his job as a waiter, and a Polish chef who worked at a top West End hotel and whose name was unpronounceable. We legered in shallow water with large pieces of bread and even larger hooks for carp, invariably catching ducks which quickly had their necks wrung before being taken by our Polish friend and transformed into delicately cooked meals.

Further transformation came one autumn day when Bob was reeling in a small perch that disappeared with a typical pike swirl and an outburst of unprintable language. Though we had fished for a year or more the presence of pike had not been considered, but we soon remedied the matter and before long were whipping out small jack up to 2·2kg (5lb) from the lake. Each pike was smacked across the head and taken away, something that would bring an outburst of conservationist cries today; but at that time food was in short supply and it was plain commonsense to fill one's belly, especially with food cooked by 'Popofski', as we had christened our Polish chef.

Battersea Park was not alone in providing local sport. Wandsworth Common lake was given a commando-style raid following the sight of a small duckling vanishing in a pike lunge and we took our best Inner London pike there, which weighed in at 3·1kg (7lb) odd. The Serpentine produced pike, as did the Royal Park Lakes which we visited by bus, grateful for free fishing in grand surroundings. Richmond contained Pen Ponds, there were Hampton Court and Bushy Park each of which contained several waters and inevitably pike. I wonder how they fare today? I have promised myself a fishing trip of nostalgia but somehow never have the time to accomplish it.

But the lean seasons quickly passed and affluence allowed better tackle at sensible prices, together with private transport – or did wages just catch up with the prices? In fact, if I were asked to define the time when pike fishing opened to the masses, who were able to travel around to find the best of the sport, I would date it from the introduction of the BSA Bantam motorcycle and the Ford Popular car.

2
Livebait and Deadbaits

It was all so simple in the now dim and distant past. Pike fishing was an extra, a bonus to the day, something for which you carried a second rod ready to set out once a few livebaits had been caught and only rarely were you disappointed. Few fishing days failed to produce the odd roach, dace or gudgeon of suitable livebait size no matter how hard the water was being fished by other anglers. Success in the coldest, hardest winter was the result of one's concentration on the quill float suspended above a ball of paste or a bunch of maggots. No bite went unnoticed and the coldest of hands would spring into action at the suggestion of an interested 'little 'un'.

Catching livebaits: as one grew older, so one became obsessed with that single thought. During those early years before the advent of deadbait fishing, livebaiting was the pivot on which pike fishing turned, the nightmare that kept you awake while you devised methods of making sure that you had enough of them to see you through the day. Even when they were safely in the keepnet the nightmare continued, for if they were to be used on subsequent days they had to be kept alive and carried around – no simple matter when the battery-driven aerator was not even a pencil line on the drawing board.

Of course, the problem was not so serious between 1 September (before which date no gentleman would dare fish for pike) and the middle of November, providing the weather stayed open and warm enough to keep small fish on the move. But an early or, worse, prolonged winter when pike fishing really came into its own also sent small fish off feed and immediately raised the value of livebaits to that of a king's ransom – and ransoms were often paid for them.

In those early days I worked and lived in London for five and a half days a week, leaving but one full day to fish and a mere half-day in which to search for those vital, elusive baits. So Saturday afternoon

27

became a hectic dash towards the Serpentine or Battersea Park lake where a stunted roach would occasionally oblige by giving itself up to a cunningly fished No 16 hook.

When the weather was hard, however, and you knew success would be out of the question, then a trip would have to be made to Fields Fishing Tackle shop in Kentish Town, where livebait were sold at 6d (2½p) each, a luxury indeed when you remembered that a dozen at least would be needed to show both pike and other pike anglers that you meant business. Then, a 24 bus took one across London, a dozen live roach in a livebait kettle in your hands and nobody would take the slightest notice. Now, I would give my eye-teeth for one of those old tinplate, green-lacquered livebait cans we used to carry our purchases in. They were flat bottomed and had steep-sloping sides and at the top were two lifting lids that allowed access and which also kept water from slopping out. Like pike floats, there was something exciting about their shape, a suggestion of pleasures to come that would instantly set daydreams alight. It was possible to obtain a deluxe version that had an inner lining of perforated zinc which aerated the water as it slopped around inside, but at £2 each they were well out of my price range and I could never afford one.

During four years spent living in London, at weekends the bath in our house was always turned over to keeping whatever livebait had been procured during the day, filled to the overflow and the cold tap left dripping all night to ensure all the fish stayed alive. Of course, there were disadvantages to this system of bait keeping, not the least being that you had to get out of bed a good half-hour earlier the following morning in order to catch each fish without damaging it before transferring it to the livebait can.

A few years ago when I visited Barrie Rickards' home I found that he had an animal drinking trough plumbed into his garage and devoted to small, lively roach, and a garden pool that housed enough healthy livebaits to make even the most conservative pikeman blasé about risking an odd one or two with rogue casts. But in the past there were no such luxuries. At regular intervals pike anglers would suffer what could only be described as desperation days, days during the course of a season when the weather was cold enough to bring a sell-out of baits from the tackle shop and there was no chance catching them oneself. At that time you used any and every fish that came to hand regardless of size or species. I have vivid memories of seeing an angler being towed along the banks of the Thames by a chub that weighed all of

28

0·7kg (1½lb). Some livebait! Each time he passed me the man shouted, 'If only the bloody thing would slow down it might just attract a pike!' Most enthusiastic pikemen have used, or seen used, perch as livebait both with and without the dorsal fin. Where did that old wives' tale come from that said the spiny fin must be removed before using a perch as livebait? I have seen an angler, on a day of white hoar frost, encouraging a ruffe to give of its best beneath the icy fringes of a riverbank. First prize, though, must go to the fisherman I saw using goldfish. At that time they were extremely rare, none having been imported during the war years. They were fetching about £2 an inch then. This chap had, then, about £16 worth of fish on a snap-tackle and another £50 worth in his livebait can!

But the desperation prize must go to an angler I watched on a Buckinghamshire gravelpit who was livebaiting with a 0·9kg (2lb) jack he had caught while spinning. I watched aghast as he set it onto an ordinary snap rig, then waited for the cast which, I knew, would surely break the tip of any rod other than a reinforced sea angling beachcaster. I felt cheated when he launched the fish out by hand and then let it work its own way towards the centre of the water, towing an outsize cork bung. An occasional pull on the line by the angler prodded it into activity if it stayed dormant for too long. I hung about for a couple of hours hoping to see a take but nothing happened; what I *did* see were some thrilling float movements. During the whole of my long pike-angling career I have never been privileged to see anything landed through the medium of a really big livebait (say above ·5kg (1lb)). And though I've heard a good many stories hinting at big baits, most have been third-person. The pike I have caught, or have seen landed – and I can include some really large fish in that number – have taken something under 170g (6oz), one of the best ever, a pike of 13·6kg (30lb) falling victim to a 10cm (4in) roach that was completely undeserving of the big hooks on which it was mounted, their weight preventing all but a few of its feeble wobbles reaching to the float above.

I do not really understand the reasoning of people who want to use livebait longer than 23cm (9in). There is some argument that big baits, struggling to get free, will send underwater vibrations over a wide area and attract pike that would not normally be aware that a livebait was on offer; and there is the theory that the bigger the bait the bigger the fish attracted visually. To be used to their full capacity big livebaits should be delivered by beachcasting rods and shock leaders to the lines if they are to be cast any distance. This is, though, counter-productive because:

a) the best-balanced rig still pulls hooks from a bait in mid-flight through line snatch, and

b) those baits that survive the cast are invariably stunned when they hit the water and quickly die.

My only experience of a bigger-than-usual livebait being used with success – and by 'success' I refer to keeping the bait alive – has been from a boat when the bait has been lowered over the side and the boat moved or allowed to drift away from it. I have no evidence that the bigger-bait-bigger-fish theory holds true. The matter of bait size is more applicable to the realm of dead and artificial baits and this is discussed later (see Chapter 3).

Some of the better livebaits I have used were trout, but this makes for an expensive day's fishing under normal circumstances in most parts of the country. The worst baits by far have always been small carp whose inherent laziness on the hook far outweighs their length of life during captivity. But I have to acknowledge that it is some years since I used livebait.

There was no particular reason behind my decision to forgo livebaiting; it was more a gradual disenchantment with this method of pike fishing. Nor am I alone in my rejection of livebaits. Many pikemen agree either in part or whole with my decision and its reasons, and have themselves followed suit.

My principal reason for giving up livebaiting centred on my being completely fed up with catching, keeping and, most of all, carting about small fish which had to be nurtured and cossetted like a first-born to ensure any chance of angling success. As each week of a season passed and winter approached, baits would become more difficult to find and I realised that I was devoting more and more of my time to catching them, quite apart from looking after them. Of course I had a supply tucked away to be drawn on, but that had its limits and I would become increasingly anxious as my stocks dwindled, to the extent that I would even unhook and keep the last bait of the day to be used on a later outing.

To be fair, I must also record that my livebaiting dislike was not only connected with what many anglers would consider to be *my* laziness. There can also be laziness on the part of livebaits – or to be more accurate an instinct for self-preservation on the part of the bait. You see, there is little or no control over a livebait once it reaches the water.

30

5 *Today's methods of keeping baits alive and attractive supercede anything used in the past. The plastic container shown here can be scrubbed clean and kept odour-free after each outing*

It might swim away immediately and settle in the midst of a weedbed, or rise to the surface and stay under the float. Or, if the float has been badly adjusted, it can hide out of view on the bottom. All of these activities will waste hours of the angler's time. Of course you can move the fish about at regular intervals, but then it ceases to have the purpose of a livebait since a dead or artificial bait might do just as well or even better. This lack of control over a livebait once it hits the water remains regardless of whether you float, leger or use a combination of those methods. And the more you pull at or recast a bait to make sure it is 'on show' the sooner it will die and become useless.

There were other reasons for my abandoning livebaiting, not the least of them being the introduction of unwanted fish into waters where they may become a nuisance, or even positively harmful to a fishery. For example, a small water in Essex, privately owned, was used by a few friends who enjoyed really excellent tench fishing with an abundance of medium-sized pike up to 7kg (15lb). The beauty of the water was its tench, the pike a bonus that one enjoyed in beautiful winter surroundings and comfort. Unfortunately the owner died and the water was leased by its new owner to a club which extracted the most from the place, few weekends going by without it being packed with anglers. Within three years most serious fishermen were giving the place a wide berth simply because any bait they offered was attacked by a host of small gudgeon.

These had been taken to the water as pike livebaits and tipped in at the end of the day when no longer required. They multiplied and became a terrible nuisance. Since then the tench have declined, probably because of the competition for food. Equally frustrating, there has been no great increase in the size of the pike. Anglers should therefore think carefully before ditching their surplus livebaits.

Finally there is the vexed question of livebait angling from the point of view of cruelty. It takes very little imagination to see that a conviction for cruelty where livebaits are concerned would rock the whole structure of field sports, not merely angling. Without going into great detail which could only provide fuel for the anti-blood sports brigade, it is therefore something we must study very carefully, but not from the point of view of a live fish being tethered as bait, because fear of being caught by a predator is something fish (and many other creatures) live with every day of their lives, but because of the way the bait is mounted. It is this that causes most concern and I must admit to a dislike of it as I have grown older.

There is, however, one way of fishing with a livebait that does not necessitate a hook being mounted into the fish's body. I first saw this method used in the late 1940s by an angler fishing one of the ponds on Hampstead Heath. The rig consisted of two double hooks mounted on a split ring that rode, rather like the saddle on a horse's back, on either side of the bait, secured in place by elastic bands under the body. I paid little attention to the idea until I saw where it had originated – in the excellent and most readable *Angling Ways* by Marshall-Hardy. I copied this rig (no tackle shop seemed to sell them) and it worked, with certain reservations, the most important being that the elastic band slipped and often broke during the cast, releasing the bait. Also, the number of hooks and their placing was clumsy and very obvious to the pike once the bait was suspended in the water. So I set to and adapted the rig with the result as shown in Fig 1 (overleaf). Here, the single hooks are mounted by their eyes through a single, large split ring, which suits baits up to about 12·5cm (5in). The hook shank is bent back into a curve that fits against the flank of the fish, and soldered to it

My favourite lure, the Guidbrod Sniper. This fish was taken by Barrie Rickards (only he could wear a coat with cuffs as frayed as those) on the Fens, a day when he and Ray Webb snaffled eighteen pike in a series of drains some a mere 3m (10ft) wide

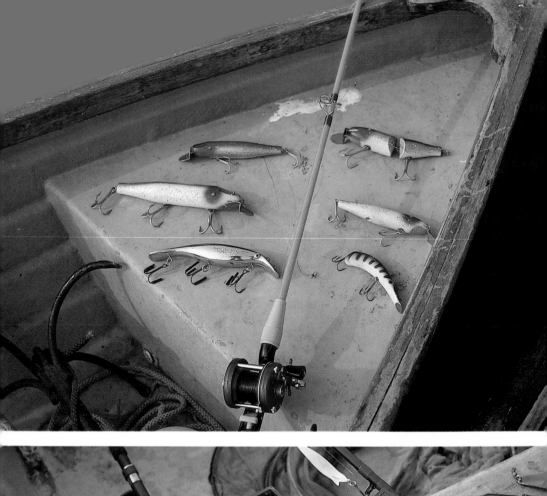

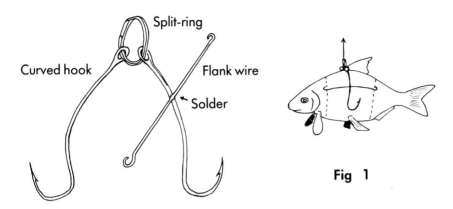

Fig 1

is a wire bar that has a loop twisted into each end. To use it, the hooks are fitted saddle-wise over the bait's dorsal fin. Then thin elastic is threaded through the eyes into the ends of the bar and tied so that the bait is secured round the body at a point behind the gills and roughly at the ventral fin.

This rig is not perfect, few are. On the plus side, the fish is held so that it has free movement without the hooks showing overmuch and placed just where the pike will seize the bait, at mid-body. On the minus side there is a slight difficulty during bait mounting (especially when the hands are cold), a need for smooth, rather short casts and the discipline to strike a little earlier than usual, at the commencement of the run and well before the bait is turned.

This means setting the hooks against the bony premaxillary area, but rather that than risk throat hooking which happens with a floating treble mounted at the gills. A good tip for setting them is to crush the barb of each hook, leaving just a slight hump instead of the big outward curve that defies penetration. Had I needed an incentive for

Plugs. These are from Fred Taylor's collection, and have accounted for dozens of pike in their lifetime. They are big, bold, and excellent workers which bring big rewards on some of the large reservoirs now opened during the closed season for game fish

Spinners have come a long way since the days of Jardine and Bickerdyke. The present-day angler can change his spinner as often as the fly fisherman changes his fly during the course of a day's sport. These spoons and Toby-type lures could cover most of the situations that the pike fisherman is likely to be faced with

giving up livebait fishing, the deadbait revolution would have provided it.

There is nothing new in the theory of using either a dead freshwater or sea fish as pike bait; it has been discussed in angling for years. But there is a world of difference between advocation and practice. I saw the suggestion again recently when I picked up a copy of the Sports and Pastime Library's *Coarse Fishing* in a secondhand bookshop. Published in 1933, revised in 1934, it stated that either a dead freshwater bait or a herring could be used for pike fishing in the same way as livebait. But the author did not give proof of pike which had been landed by the method.

Anglers at that time did not believe that a dead fish would attract a pike and the suggestion was seen as another piece of angling folklore. It took anglers like Fred Taylor to achieve success with the method. His published accounts showed that success could be obtained with saltwater baits in freshwater fisheries. But I had caught pike on deadbaits long before the method became popular in the late 1950s. I had caught pike when legering for eels on the Thames around Penton Hook and Hampton Court, using a dead bleak or roach mounted on a large single hook tied to gimp, the type sold by Woolworths and capable of holding an ocean-going liner without breaking. When I told friends, I found that it had happened to them as well. We none of us had the sense to realise that this was something quite new, the making

6 *The simple deadbait rig for float, leger or paternoster fishing that the author uses in preference to all other multihook varieties. The treble hooks are Size 10, and the swivel contains ball-bearings to cope with the twists and turns of a hooked fish. The pliers are a Hardy model*

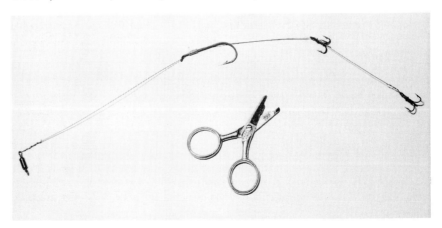

of a revolution in pike fishing. After all, who in those days ever seriously considered legering for pike?

What confused us was the spasmodic nature of the captures, which always came in the warm months of June, July and August. Had we used the baits through a few winter months we would have achieved fame and fortune. Most of our pike then were caught on deadbaits mounted and used with spinning tackles of one sort or another.

Without the benefit of domestic deep-freezers to preserve a supply of baits to last the winter the only way was to buy them ready preserved in jars, or pickle them oneself. That meant catching a supply of small, similar-sized roach and dace which were packed into screw-top jars and covered with preserving liquid, usually a dilute solution of formaldehyde. It was great fun and we caught pike with these baits but only, however, when they were spun, and never when left lying in the water as deadbaits are today.

Our success was probably due to the way the preservative toughened the skin of the bait until it was strong enough to withstand repeated casting and rapid retrieval. The mounts were lead-weighted or metal cased and bristled with trebles, their weight making them bump along the bottom. Poor construction, or perhaps bad mounting, usually gave them a fish-attracting wobble instead of the rhythmic spin we wanted.

But the art of pure deadbaiting developed and eventually became the battle of the rigs, so that right up to this day little energy and time have been spent on a study of the bait itself. The appearance of the bait attracts pike and we should concentrate on making it look as natural as possible without impediments. The average angler does not consider the bait's condition, nor the importance of size, shape or species. The most successful anglers, who catch pike when conditions are against them, spend time and money on their baits and in keeping and carrying them.

Over 70 per cent of pike anglers prefer sea fish simply because the supply is easy and convenient. They also buy more than enough for a day's fishing, those remaining being thrown in to 'feed the pike' at the end of the day. In fact all they do is pollute the water for those who follow and give a bad name to anglers in general by leaving the area littered with their rubbish.

My local fishmonger is also a pike fisherman and so I am allowed to select my baits. Size is important, and colour and firmness are qualities badly needed when I want herring and mackerel. One cannot pick and choose from a tray of sprats, the only thing to do is get them home and sort them out there. Baits like these will be more attractive when fresh, not only from appearance but from the odour they give off. Old mackerel do not exude those drops of oil which rise to the surface above the bait, revealing its position. When possible I try to get to the coast and buy mackerel sold within a few hours of capture. When taken from the freezer and defrosted they produce twice the amount of oil that slab-bought fish do, and catch more pike.

My method of freezing and carrying baits takes time but is worth the effort. I wash them thoroughly in cold water and dry them. A newspaper is laid open and strips cut from it the same width of the fish to be frozen. The first fish is laid on it, and the paper folded over before the next bait is laid head to tail; more fish are folded in, ready for the freezer. I pack sprats in sixes, herring and mackerel in fours, leaving even bigger fish whole. Then the rolls of bait are put in freezer bags and sealed before being quick-frozen. The bags keep any taint from other food stored there and when required they come out easily.

Deep-frozen baits should be de-frosted before use. In cold water a frozen bait has litttle attraction other than shape. Odour to which pike respond is lacking while the bait is ice-bound and in winter it may not even de-frost in the water, losing most of its attraction. Baits which are not used should be inspected carefully for signs of deterioration before being put back in the freezer. The condition of the eyes is important, I have found that pike seem not to be interested if the eyes are missing or blanked out. It might be to do with a predator watching the eyes of its prey for signs of response. Even a plug which has not had the eyes painted on seems to lack some of its attraction for pike.

Are sea fish better baits than freshwater species? It depends on the water. Some gravel pit pike fall regularly to sea fish and it may be because they have been conditioned to those baits. This seems true of the well-fished pits. Some years ago while walking round the North Met pits at Cheshunt I checked on the baits and found that all the anglers were using sea baits, mostly herring. It meant that a feeding pike had no choice. But when I fished a small lake in the Welsh mountains I was the first angler there in years, certainly before deadbaiting came in, and I had immediate success with small sprats, a food alien to the fish there. So on the water new to you, go prepared to 'fish and see' – and take a selection of baits, freshwater and salt.

7 *The use of deadbaits revolutionised pike fishing, although it had been advocated for years. It is still no passport to automatic success because few anglers take the care to select and present their bait to its best advantage. From the author's experience the herring, shown here, is a poor offering when compared with the mackerel – and some freshwater fish are more effective deadbaits than the sea species*

3
Spinners and Plugs

So far as the world of spinning is concerned I must have been a late developer. Today's angling youngsters take to it easily and believe in it, but in my youth one never gave the method a thought because we just did *not* have faith in it! Nothing would convince us that a large chunk of metal slung out into the water and pulled back to the bank would incite a pike to do other than swim like the dickens in the opposite direction and away from the disturbance. Why did we act and think that way? Probably because so much of our time was occupied with fishing for the delicate species such as roach and carp where stealth was everything; and also possibly because of the big enemy we faced in those impecunious times – lack of money.

It must be remembered too that the spinners of the pre-war years and the immediate post-war era were hefty items of tackle. They had changed little from the days of Jardine and Bickerdyke and seldom weighed less than 57g (2oz), sometimes reaching 113g (4oz) or more. This weight was necessary, for without it one could not cast; the fixed-spool reel and the multiplier were in their infancy and were well out of the price range of the majority of anglers; added to which these reels were not matched by rods of a correct weight and length.

When cast over the water those heavy spinners had to turn a Nottingham-type drum well filled with plaited silk line which (in theory at least) was less likely to kink than twisted silk, plus some extra weight above the trace in the form of a Jardine spiral lead or one of those boat-shaped Wye leads. But there was not, as I have said, a great deal of spinning done. I cannot recall watching an angler spinning on more than one occasion, and that left me unimpressed. Even the gift of a box of assorted spinning monstrosities failed to nudge me into the style and eventually I ceased carrying the unwanted weight with me when I went fishing.

40

In that period the most popular of the primitive lures was the kidney spoon, silver on one side and red the other with the traditional, hook-rusting tuft of red wool laid round the shank of the end treble, an offer, the adverts insisted, that no self-respecting pike was supposed to be able to refuse.

There were spoons in plenty, both copper and silver; Hardy's had one on the market which, if I remember correctly, was either covered with or manufactured completely from mother-of-pearl, and naturally the price matched its beauty. But the worst of the lot in those days of brute force and angling grit was without doubt the slotted Devon Minnow. As I write there is one before me, the price still on it – 3s 11d in 'old' money and about 20p now – if you could buy one.

This specimen is still stitched onto the card on which it was sold after leaving the factory and the three tiny trebles plus two flying sets – allowed to revolve outside the body-shell itself – catch on everything that gets near enough. The ability of this lure to 'keyhole' while being cast, a problem brought about by the weight added to the trace to help achieve distance, was some 75 per cent of all casts made and some of the colourful bad language I learned as a boy came from an elderly angler using a Slotted Devon while spinning for sea trout on the Sussex Ouse.

With the end of World War II I eventually moved to London and found that there were larger waters available to me than had been the case when I lived in Sussex. This gave me the opportunity to give the spinning method a try while piking on the Thames but I quickly abandoned the idea, not because of faith in the style but simply because of the problems of casting. To achieve any distance, and distance was supposed to be all-important, one had to strip line off the wooden Nottingham reel and lay it on the ground. The coils of line then had to be reversed, after which the cast could be attempted.

This was fine in theory but in practice every piece of grass, twig or leaf would snag the line and then wedge firmly in the first rod ring as the cast was made, bringing the process to a sudden halt. The lure would flail round and back towards the angler with potentially damaging results. More time was spent unravelling tangles than was ever spent fishing.

Then faith and interest was restored during the early fifties with the launching on the market of an item called the Adaptacast. This was a metal attachment fitted between the reel fitting and the reel saddle, being fastened by clips that were mounted either side of a simple swivel. To make a cast one just turned the reel so that the drum faced forwards instead of in line with the rod handle. From this position and provided that the drum was filled to the lip with line a cast could be made which allowed the line to run off the rim of the drum in the way a fixed-spool reels works. The main difference, of course, was that the average fixed-spool reel was very expensive – a fiver – in those days whereas the Adaptacast cost 2s 6d (12½p).

The first pike I saw taken by a spinner with the aid of the Adaptacast came from the Broadwater, a stretch of water in the grounds of Windsor Castle that runs across a wide bend of the Thames. I was fishing as a guest of one of the Royal coachmen who prevented a blank day by mounting a large silver spoon and casting it underneath overhanging bushes against the opposite bank, from where he caught five pike in nearly as many minutes. What made the performance even more memorable was that it was nearly dark when the fish came on feed, a time of day not normally associated with notable winter success. But this subject will be elaborated upon later.

That event was enough and I began, very cautiously, to try spinning, although not convinced that the style would work; I realised that some care would be needed, for the replacement of two or three lost spinners represented a tidy sum in those days. So I compromised and began spinning not with artificial lures but with deadbaits.

Any angler today would be laughed at if he were discovered using some of the deadbait tackles of the late forties and fifties. There were still a few of the Crocodile mounts being sold, things rather like gin-traps that snapped shut on the body of a fair-sized bait and allowed a cluster of flying trebles to revolve with the bait as it was retrieved. But far more useful – and much cheaper – were the Archer flights, spinning mounts that held small fish, sprats or prawns, and these were very effective, depending of course on the supply and toughness of the fish to be used as deadbaits.

Through the summer and autumn months there were never any problems in obtaining deadbaits, for bleak, dace or small roach were plentiful and could be caught, killed and freshly mounted on the spot. These would hold together for a good number of casts before disintegrating and falling apart through the stress of casting and retrieving. But the winter months were an entirely different proposition. Then, we tended to use sea fish such as sprats and herring bought from the fishmonger's slab but they soon broke apart, lasting for one or two casts at the most.

The problem was solved by preserving summer-caught baits by pickling them in formaldehyde, a process which toughened them and provided freshwater fish deadbaits when there were none to be caught along the banks. But those who have not smelt baits steeped in formaldehyde have no conception of the all-pervading stink that is produced. In a very short time and regardless of any amount of care taken in carrying baits to the waterside that sickly-sweet smell would quickly find its way throughout the contents of a tacklebag, including one's sandwiches. Clothing would smell of it and a cloud seemed to follow one everywhere – and naturally the fish were not overkeen on the odour either. Some were caught, although during the seasons when I used formaldehyde as a preservative I shudder to think how many became aware of the taint and stopped short as they approached the bait.

There were a few cheap and cheerful spinners on the market whose prices did not break the bank. Most were spoons and there was that outstanding Mackerel Spinner that over the years had probably landed as many fish of all species than any other lure I can recall. Another lure of those days was the Wagtail, a proven killer. This odd-looking piece of rubber with its single tail-mounted treble was especially successful in weirpools on the Thames and was included in the standard equipment of the Thames trout angler.

In time I took another piece of tackle from the armoury of the trouter, the four-treble trace which was used to mount a bleak in such a way that when retrieved it would spin through the water without metal vanes or other aids (see Photograph 8). The secret lay in giving the bait's tail a soft twist before mounting the end treble into it, and this was very difficult to do for if not done properly the bleak would swoop rather than spin through the water. This did not, however, make any great depreciation in the effectiveness of the bait when used for weirpool pike, for there were days when the swoop would score over the spin!

I would probably have remained in that particular groove of spinning for many a season had I not taken a book out of my local public library that totally revised my ideas on spinning and which was to make this special branch of angling my favourite above all others. This book was *The Science of Spinning for Salmon and Trout* and I read and re-read it before pestering every library and secondhand bookshop in the district until I had not only read but possessed every book that its author wrote. That man was Alexander Wanless.

What a character he must have been! So definite in what he wrote, so sure, and years ahead of his time where the technique of spinning is concerned. I immediately adopted his method of preserving baits, which enabled the formaldehyde to be reduced to the minimum, and then I settled into the serious business of lightweight spinning using the tactics he described but employing the modern tackle that was now appearing on the market. The mass-produced fixed-spool reel, monofilament lines, streamlined anti-kink devices, Alasticum traces to replace that dreaded wire gimp that was as useful as a balsawood leger weight – all became available at prices within the reach of nearly every angler. And there were also glass-fibre rods, and spinners in shapes, forms and colours never before imagined.

The enthusiasm and belief in fine tackle and tactics I received from reading Wanless has lasted to this day. I have even made a counterpart to his ultra-light spinning tackle and have used it with great success in selected waters, taking care to use the rod and reel in scale with the delicate lines needed to complete a balance. The rod was a 2·1m (7ft) No 4 fly rod with about 7·6cm (3in) lopped from its tip, thus stiffening its action. There was a traditional solid cork handle and special rod rings made by the rod-maker to balance the outfit.

The reel I chose was a closed-face matchfishing model, reason dictating that on the small waters where the rod would be used there would be obstructions in plenty and bankside herbage in abundance. It was a sound judgement and this lightweight rod and reel, balanced with lines from 1·3–2·2kg (3–5lb), has given me some excellent sport, often from places where the traditional heavyweight pike tackle just would not fit, nor score.

But I did not entirely give up spinning with deadbaits and still use the method today. It is cheap, interesting and natural – especially from the point of view of the pike, for many of my biggest specimens have been taken by deadbait spinning. I no longer use that foul chemical formaldehyde to preserve baits, nor do I freeze those I intend to spin with for it makes them just as soft, tender and liable to break up during casting as the 'fresh' bait from the fishmonger when they thaw out. My current method of preserving is to put a quantity of silica gel into the bottom of a casserole dish (kept specially for that purpose), then set a wire frame, cut and shaped to fit the dish, above the crystals so that the baits can be spread across the wire without touching the gell. Silica gel can be obtained from most DIY shops, it is also advertised as an aid for curing dampness.

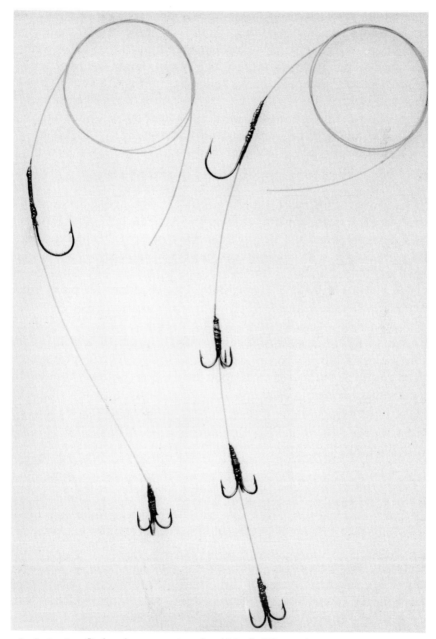

8 *Spinning flights for mounting dead bleak. These rigs are a pattern originally tied in monofilament for Thames trouting, but they are easy to manufacture in fine Alasticum and thin wire trebles. This rig is deadly in weirpools and fastwater stretches*

Once in the dish the lid is sealed with adhesive tape and the container is set aside for 48 hours. At the end of that time the baits will have dried out, the gel having absorbed their moisture; the now wet gel can then be put in a warm place to dry out, ready for reuse in the future. I prefer baits that are sizeable (size-limit-wise), such as bleak, dace and rudd, to the smaller species of sea fish though beggars can't be choosers and I sometimes tend to forget to obtain the baits until it is too late to collect sufficient before the winter sets in.

The dried baits are put on to paper out in the open in a place sheltered from the wind and then they are simply sprayed on both sides with either a thin cellulose varnish or a colour of one's choice. By using those aerosol cans of car colours that are obtainable from motor accessory shops, the job only takes a few seconds. If a colour has been used it pays to add a final seal of clear cellulose varnish which will stop the paint flaking. Then the baits can be packed into plastic bags in sixes or so and placed in the freezer until wanted. This tends to put a bloom on the colours through moisture being absorbed into the paint but it makes no difference to the ability of the baits to attract fish.

This method of preservation is a bit complex, but it is one which provides some excellent baits that wobble when mounted by the shirt-button method (see Chapter 5), and spin well on a sprat mount that can still be purchased from good tackle shops or made at home by the average handyman. It will last and last through the most difficult and damaging of casts that have to be made in rugged areas. I never think of tackling some of the very fast water where I fish for pike without a supply of these home-made baits.

A number of years back I became convinced that spinning should be more of a science than the chuck-it-and-chance-it 'style' adopted by many pike anglers. So far as they were concerned any spinner would do and the farther it could be cast and the longer the retrieve took or was made to last then the greater was their chance of success. By then I had worked out the 'count-down' method of retrieval, using an increasing number of seconds after the bait had entered the water before starting the retrieve. This meant that the lure was always working at different levels in the water until the taking depth had been established. But I was extremely unhappy at not being certain what the fish saw as the lure was worked through its field of vision. Then one day in the early seventies the chance to experiment and solve the mystery came when I met that fine pike angler Barrie Rickards.

Barrie had access to a flume tank – an aquarium some 9m (30ft) long through which a flow of water could be introduced, and which had a bottom of sand and gravel. On a day when the tank was not in use officially we arranged a series of lights along the tank and a camera set facing one side. The idea was to photograph each type of spinner as it was drawn through the water and against the current. The camera was operated using a slow shutter speed, allowing the blurred image of the passing spinner to be recorded as it crossed the plane of the film. In other words, I wanted to record what the fish saw underwater and not what the human eye saw from above.

In retrospect, we were lucky that Barrie was not electrocuted that day. The lights were ordinary photofloods, which were balanced on top of the tank to represent sunlight falling on the water. Barrie was standing, using the bottom joint of a rod with reel attached to draw each lure through the angle of the camera lens, and he would have received a lethal electric shock had one of the lights fallen into the water.

When the film was processed and printed the results were staggering. We immediately realised that leaf spinners produce light patterns through the moving edge of the blade *and nowhere else*, whereas Toby-type lures, those elongated spoons, produce vivid figure-of-eight patterns that reflect light with each move. But of the greatest importance of all was the realization that all those pretty colours, eyes, scale patterns and so on, whether attached or simulated, are useless when it comes to viewing a spinning lure from the point of view of the pike. All one could see was a blur, and nothing else. Vertical stripes on a lure gave no added attraction, but lures whose shapes were broken with horizontal stripes along the body broke up into more light patterns than a plain coloration and were more visible. After our day's photography we quickly revised our ideas on what spinners should and should not be included in a tackle box.

Now my choice of lures is catholic. I am never without a Mepps in the bag, this lure has a big leaf blade that produces a big glint and I like the hooks that are attached to the end of the body. Neither am I ever without a selection of spoons in various sizes – all home made and every bit as good as the shop-bought models. Here I add a note of caution to all those anglers who like to make their own lures: some are worth the effort, some are not.

When I took to spinning I made a quantity of Colorado spoons that looked ideal but no matter how I tried I could not get wire of sufficient temper to prevent the lure body from jamming as it revolved during a retrieve. Then when at last I did get the tempered wire I did not have the tools to make the small loops, so I was back to square one. Now my spinner making centres around plain spoons, either from the 'table' kind or those cut and beaten into shape from sheet metal, and Toby-type lures made in the same way. Making one's own lures enables the angler to produce the sizes that can be used on trout reservoirs when pike culling takes place and where the rule is nothing under 12·7cm (5in) may be used – and one suddenly finds a world shortage of spinners of that size when they are required.

Toby lures are always good, but also successful are the Shakespeare Catcher and the ABU Atom, both manufactured in the same style and both with a hammered, not painted, scale pattern that really does reflect some glint during the retrieve. I have already mentioned the humble but excellent Mackerel Spinner and to this I must add the Quill Minnow, either the natural or plastic kind and of course the Irish Minnow which is the same as the Quill Minnow but much heavier. It is grand for spinning in the faster rivers, where it is used by game fishermen. There are plenty more, some rarely seen, though a few models are still in production. I always poke around in tackle shops for effective and killing 'old-timers' and often find them – the Vibro and Voblex, for instance.

Which are the spinners that I do not like? Well, the Devon Minnows, not that there is any reflection in my description of the Slotted Devon mentioned at the beginning of this chapter, but simply because I have had little success with them, which is probably only to be expected: when viewed in the flume tank this lure scores a near-zero on the marking system when its light reflecting qualities are studied. I also have an inbuilt hate of lightweight lures, for to add weight always leads to casting problems and also to fish taking a lunge at the weight instead of at the lure itself.

My preference in colours for spinning? Golds, greens, silvers are the best and most of the better fish I have caught have had some of these colours on the successful lure. You will have noted that the colours I have given are exactly those found on pike and most other coarse fish. Blues, browns and reds are not on my preferred list but strangely they do attract fish when on plug lures.

Before moving on to discuss plugs in pike fishing it may be as well to consider the trends in the design of today's spinners. Once there was nothing but varying weight from which to choose when selecting spinners, but today there is a trend towards movement and not just a straightforward spin or wobble. I have acquired a packet of spinners and other lures through the courtesy of Bomber Bait Company of Texas, U.S., including some exotic items that are enthusiastically described as Buzz or Bushwacker Baits and these are quite unlike anything that is on sale in this country, a situation I am quite convinced will soon change.

Basically, Buzz Baits are wire booms set at angles, the apex of which is attached to the line (see Fig 2). On one boom are set the spinning blades, usually two and not armed with hooks. On the other boom is what can only be described as a miniature octopus complete with head

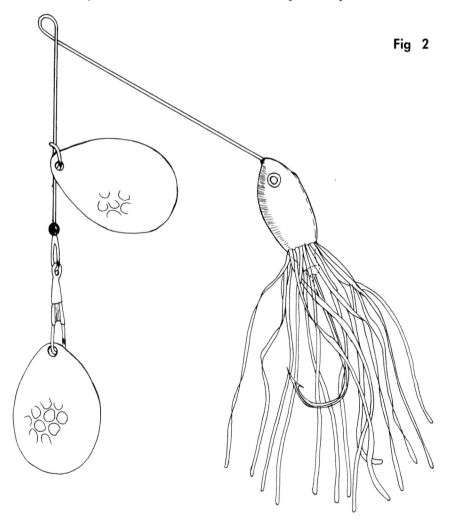

Fig 2

and skirt of plastic fronds in garish colours, armed with one or more large, well-tempered hooks. When drawn through the water, this lure provides a combination of attraction through the movement of the plastic fronds which wave in the current and produce vibrations, plus some attractive light patterns from the leaf spinner that revolves alongside the hook.

Once you have recovered from the initial shock at the apparent clumsiness and garish finish of this lure you will quickly discover two important advantages. One is that the whole thing is semi-snagless, the arms collapsing and sliding over solid underwater objects that can be met during a deep retrieve, while the weight of the lure ensures that those deep and awkward holes are fished properly. Secondly, the lure really does take fish, especially during the summer months when there is a lot of weed in which pike prefer to lie, with the lure collapsing (as described) and breaking free to ensure that heavy strain is taken from the angler's pocket.

Another innovation for the spin-fisherman's armoury is the Vibro Sonic Bat (Fig 3) which came to my notice during a recent trip to Australia. The illustration shows the outline of this lure which is made

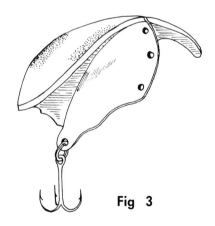

Fig 3

Right
Fastwater fishing in Wales. Here the drop-sprat is being used with lightweight tackle on a small stream that produces pike up to 3·6kg (8lb) or so. Note that the angler is rigged for a roving-style, and may cover several miles of stream during a day

from fairly heavy metal. The depth at which it will work is decided upon by fixing the line to one of three holes at the front of the lure, and this dictates the angle at which the front will tilt and ultimately run. Once it is working there is a definite swinging action from this unusual bat-shaped lure which gives not only a visual attraction but whose vibrations also produce sound waves, forming a combination that makes a real killer. Like the Buzz lure, one wonders just how long it will be before both these excellent lures appear on the English market and take us yet another step away from the age-old spoon shape.

Visual attraction and attraction through vibration underwater — both are now acknowledged as standard essentials required by the successful spinner. But there is one other item that is as yet undeveloped, and that is scent. The Americans realised this many years ago and used bacon strips, sold ready preserved, which were attached to trebles on a lure. As the lure was worked through the water the strips trailed eel-wise through the wake left by the spinner. It is a method that has somehow never taken on in this country, but I can testify that it works — and there is plenty of scope for experiment too.

My trials have been with lobworms, bacon rind, mackerel strips and — best of all, preserved or when freshly caught — sandeels fastened behind the body of the spinner. All of them have caught fish, and often when the spinner on its own has been a dismal failure. Currently I am experimenting with long, thin strips of foam plastic soaked in pilchard oil: the results so far are good but marred by the unpleasant smell of the oil, which also gets off the hands and onto everything that one touches.

Of late there has been an increasing interest shown in fishing for pike using flies, and I suspect that this has been occasioned by the numbers of pike that seem to be inhabiting some of our better trout reservoirs and which attach themselves to the fly fisherman's artificials without invitation. Why the pike take these special artificials is a mystery for the flies look — and cast — like nothing on earth; presumably the pike see them as small fish and lunge instinctively. But there are many other 'one-offs' like that, including jigs and poppers, more items that have served an apprenticeship in the States and which are slowly and gently filtering into Britain.

Summer specials. A selection of plugs that work the surface to perfection though many anglers tend to overlook them for deep workers. These have scored on the Thames time after time for me and are especially useful for working when a boat is used

Jigs are by far the most successful of the two lures, the jig being manufactured from a metal body moulded round a large single hook and adorned with feathers. It can be cast on light tackle with deadly accuracy and it is about the only lure that I know which can tempt a pike and hoist it out of a seemingly safe holt.

Poppers, on the other hand, are cork or plastic-bodied artificial insects that float on the surface; they are complete with legs and so on made from thin rubber strands that move to the lightest touch. I obtained some from the States which were on the small side, but with a specimen before me it was easy to make a scaled-up model that would do for pike fishing. The popper is an ideal bait that can be worked on small streams, over heavy weedbeds, anywhere in fact where a floating bait would be the only chance of making contact with a pike. I once watched a jack of about 2·7kg (6lb) repeatedly take newts as they swam up to the surface for air, and I have seen pike swirl and take bumble bees off the surface. However, I have no desire to make imitations of newts or bumble bees even though pike take them occasionally.

Where do we go with spinning in the future? I think that we shall see small, computerised baits that before long will give movement, exude scent and produce massive light reflection. It would not be considered fair angling at the moment – but then neither were bite indicators when they first appeared on the market. There is no doubt about it – anglers of the future who have grown up alongside the mighty microchip will accept that kind of lure as quite normal and use it without hesitation. And before those comments are dismissed as rubbish, remember that if 30 years ago I had said man would walk on the moon that suggestion would have been found just as unacceptable.

Today's plugs are representative of the advances that can and will be made in modern angling design. As I write, in front of me is a set of the original Jock Scotts, wooden plugs that looked somewhat like that old-fashioned clothes peg, but which were fitted with a treble hook underneath the body. To that round body, at the belly and in front of the hook could be attached a variety of interchangeable weights to take the plug down to the depth at which it was required to work, the weight a fore-runner of the diving vane one can see on present-day models.

I have fished with the original Jock Scott and it is an excellent lure, although rather slow in its movement and it is as equally capable of taking good fish as its modern counterpart. In fact, some of the

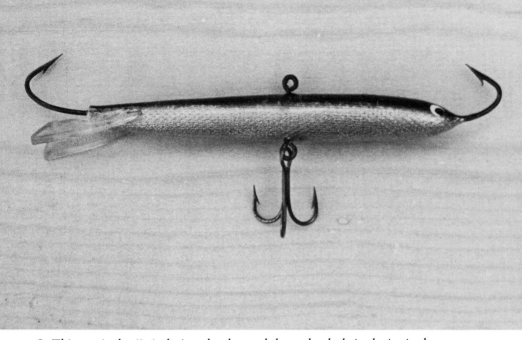

9 *This particular jig is designed to be used through a hole in the ice in the USA, but it is equally successful in Britain. It is self-weighed. Jigs come in many shapes and sizes*

modern plugs I have seen and used are not a patch on the old-timers, not from the design angle but from the standard of workmanship, which on some modern plugs is appalling. I have seen plugs for sale at enormous prices but with badly centred vanes, poor hook mounts and atrocious-quality hooks. But there is no problem in changing weights with the modern diving vane that replaced them, and present-day plug design means that it can be buoyant so that it can float to the surface, then be made to sink when required, whereas the old Jock Scott sank without trace or warning if one was not careful.

It is wise to pay a shade more for the best branded names because you will get hard-wearing, balanced lures that will catch fish – not just the fisherman.

To be perfectly honest, I would prefer a day's plug fishing to one of spinning. The plug is such a versatile weapon when piking, and more especially on the difficult waters where one can only make a straight retrieve with a spinner and hope that it will not snatch or snag. But one can take a deep-diving plug with a floating body on such waters and it can be made to work down into the depths of a weed-and-snag-ridden gravel pit, for instance, and when the snags start to become apparent the lure can be allowed to float to the surface, pulled over the danger area and sent down to the depths again.

There are also plugs for working various depths and even on the surface itself. The latter area is one frequently forgotten or even ignored by plugmen, yet in summer and early autumn there are good pike to be found over the weeds in the shallows and from tiny streams in places where many anglers would not even consider fishing. Sadly there is a serious dearth of classic plugs on the market now, almost as if the surge of interest that occurred in the late sixties and early seventies ran out of impetus. So bad is the situation that I now study a water, look in my plugbox, and then think twice about selecting one of my favourite patterns – say a Guidbrod Sniper – simply because the chances of obtaining a replacement are practically nil if it should be lost.

There has been a subtle change in the shape of plugs in the past ten years or so. Time was when the plug was elongated, probably jointed and offered several sets of treble hooks; now, the plug will tend to have a single body, deep in the chest, tailing towards the waist and end treble and will appear relatively awkward and chunky when compared with the older models. Many new plugs have a sonic device, normally a round piece of metal enclosed within a hollow part of the body and which is designed to rattle about in the space. It is claimed that the vibrations produced during the retrieve have the effect of bringing fish near. Unfortunately the experiments that I have made failed to convince me that there is any advantage in this system; in fact, more vibrations will come from a vane or spinner attached to the body externally and pushing or pulling water in its passage.

Does a plug that is a good representation of a particular fish have any more chance of success than one of the eye-catching models that generally grace the shelves of tackle shops? For years I was convinced that it made not the slightest difference, but recently I obtained some plugs from the States that are near-exact replicas of the freshwater crayfish (Photograph 10). Fished tail-first in a series of jerks much as the real crustacean makes as it moves through the water, these plugs certainly score above others, even in waters that so far as I know have never held crayfish. On the other hand, in those same waters I have caught pike with a double-jointed plug half of which was painted red, the other white and which in no way represented any known creature – but not with the same regularity as the near-perfect imitation!

10 *Crayfish like this king-sized specimen are not pike food, but small ones have been found in pike stomachs. This crustacean needs pure, running water over a gravelly bed, but it is becoming scarce due to pollution. Remarkably accurate plastic copies are used as lures and when used backwards in sink-and-draw fashion they are constant killers*

There has been a move in the USA and Australia recently to manufacture plugs that are shaped like real bait-fish, with colours in the plastic that are really startling in their realism and clarity. I have used them and find that they are good pike attractors, but – again – I have this intense feeling that any lure is only as good as the faith with which it is fished. I have also noticed a trend towards bigger plugs, which work well, especially on large reservoirs and lakes. It is something that could certainly be emulated by the manufacturers of spinners. When large expanses of water come into discussion one must then consider trolling, trailing, or just plain towing a lure behind a boat. At one time this technique was frowned upon in the world of angling but of late trolling has had some followers who have achieved grand results on large expanses of water where annual pike culls are held. At Bewl Bridge, in Kent, I have taken bigger and more pike by using a trolled lure, either a plug or a plain spoon, than by the traditional method of casting and retrieving, but only, I hasten to add, in areas where the water is deep enough and sufficiently clear to allow the method to be used without constant snagging.

It is usual to use the artificial and spin or plug-fish during the day, but there has been a recent move to use the same methods during the early hours of darkness where on some of the bigger reservoirs there has been a response. It is done only in areas where there is regular fishing activity and then not after 2300hrs or so regardless of the weather. Perhaps it suggests that pike move into well-fished areas after dark to forage for what has been left or thrown into the water by anglers, but I have no proof of this.

The fish taken at night have been big, by daytime standards at least, and there has been no need to use the Flectolite material or highly polished metalwork one would imagine would be needed to reflect a light pattern of some kind in the dark. Even the phases of the moon appear to make no difference, but, then, I know of one good water where bigger-than-usual pike can be taken after dark, the area being well-illuminated by lights from a nearby roadbridge.

So does the apparent lack of need for light supply proof that vibration after dark is all-important? But then, again, I have had success with a Mackerel Spinner, which would not normally be high on my list of night-time lures although it does produce some reasonable vibrations. I have made attempts to discuss all these matters with many anglers along the banks but have met with no response, and bearing in mind the dire penalties that are threatened by Water Authorities in some parts of the country for fishing after dark their reticence can only be expected!

To close this chapter, I am convinced that a re-think and some research into the matter of pike spinning and plug fishing after dark could open up a new facet to the sport and bring some startling catches. But not, perhaps, in my lifetime.

4
Fast Waters

Ask a pike angler to join you on an exclusive stillwater fishery for a day's sport and he will probably bowl you over in his headlong dash to get tackle and bait. His eagerness will know no bounds. But approach that same angler to be your companion on a similarly exclusive fast-water fishery, one of those where the current pushes hard, and it is a near-certainty that he will find an excuse, or if he does accept he will hesitate and then pick your brains as how you will be fishing that water.

Why should this be? Is it due to his laziness, lack of faith in the water, or in his ability to employ tactics that will catch fish or even to keep a bait in a swim where the water is very fast? All these reasons possibly account for some of the lack of interest in fishing fast water; but the real reason is usually just a lack of practice in balancing bait, tackle and style to the demands of speedy water facing the angler.

What is meant by 'fast water'? Examples are the Hampshire Avon and the Welsh Wye, two waters typically fast and in different parts of Britain. Of course, fast water can occur on slow rivers, the weirpools of the Thames, or the feeder-streams which flow through high ground before joining the main flow of large rivers. All rivers in flood conditions can be very fast, and these are the times when many anglers stay at home, leaving their tackle standing in a corner and forgetting about fishing until the flood abates.

This attitude to rivers in flood is a defeatism which I have never understood. In spite of the fact that many rivers flood every winter the angler must be aware of the topography of a favourite water well enough even though some of its identifying features may be underwater. I have a feeling that pikemen mentally adopt the attitude that fish leave the river altogether in flood conditions and that if they went fishing they would catch nothing.

11 *One is seldom disappointed with a day's fishing at a weir for the fish will be there summer or winter. It is necessary for the angler to understand the topography of the bottom of the pool, and he must be prepared to lose tackle after floodwaters, which bring large amounts of debris into the pool*

Let us examine this latter phenomenon and consider it thoroughly before dealing with waters that constantly flow quickly. Think of your favourite water and mentally study it. You will know every place where a pike has shown in the past and where all the areas where fish are likely to lie, places where a pike will hold if no better place is available. Now imagine a flood occurring, with hard, coloured water pushing downstream: if you were a pike where would you go? If you thought that the pike would leave their normal holts and run for shelter you would in most cases be quite wrong.

Every pike fights for the place it holds in the river and it will never abandon that holt because it would be taken and the original pike would not be able to reoccupy it. The very shape of a pike enables it to hold position in a good pressure of water, the streamlining and the powerful tail enabling it to resist or, rather, avoid much of the current (see Photograph 12). A move will only be made as a last resort, when the flow is such that it is nigh impossible to remain stationed there because the silt, mud and debris being forced downstream becomes a hazard to the fish, especially to its sensitive and delicate gill structure.

Now, if such a move is forced upon the pike what kind of place will it seek? Certainly, it will not be to dead slack water. Pike that inhabit moving water seem suspicious of dead areas and generally avoid them, whether through 'fear' of being visible to predators, through excessive amounts of silt and mud settling, or because they are uneasy in a strange environment. Any angler who fishes those areas will usually earn the blank that he so often gets.

There is only one place to seek pike in normally slow-flowing waters that are flooded and that is to look for water where the speed lies between that which is streaming fast and completely still. Fish those places even though they be only a few feet deep and weed and debris make it difficult to keep the bait in position, forcing repeated casting. The fishing is hard, sometimes boring and, if the weather is very wet and cold, really miserable, but that is the only solution to the problem so far as my experience is concerned.

This is illustrated by a day that I recall as I search through my diary to substantiate these assertions. I was fishing a small game fishery not far from where Izaak Walton used to roam while instilling fear among

12 These two pike were caught from a fast stream and are the shape that the author prefers. In such waters pike have to work hard for their food, and in consequence become muscular and put up a spirited resistance when hooked

the local milkmaids. The watercourse normally caters for an overflow from a canal system and is governed by a large sluicegate at its head. During times of flood that barrier opens automatically and a strong head of water pushes downstream through the fishery.

On the day in question I tackled up with two rods (my maximum) and before starting to fish I walked the banks to check on the area generally. Instead of trying to express the speed of the flow in knots, it would be better if I described it as a fast walking pace, one that would be difficult to sustain even on flat, open banks. I saw that there were near-slack areas of water just before each bend in the river and since there were five or six such bends there was enough to provide good ground for the day's sport. I compromised with my usual tackle and adapted a method that old Bickerdyke would have described as 'tight-corking or laying-on': in other words I put extra weight on the line above the trace, used a slimline float and fished the slack water, resting the rod so that line, float and weight were at an angle to the rod tip, with the deadbait on the bottom. The bale-arm of the reel was open and the line looped under an elastic band that gripped tightly around the rod just above the handle. This is a delicate method, provided that one remembers to keep out of sight before, during and especially after the cast.

Both rods were set up in this fashion, using sprats as bait, then I sat back and waited. In two hours I had made three moves without even the suggestion of a swirl, let alone a take, so I opted for the easy way out, took my tackle and adjourned to the keeper's hut. This was a cosy affair with a fire roaring in a cast-iron stove that filled one corner. Before settling to make tea and fry some sausages I set the rod out right in front of the hut where there was a dead-straight stretch of water, laying-on as before just 1·8m (6ft) or so from the bank in water well under a metre (3·2ft) deep with a steady but not fast flow. I could see my floats from the window. But before the frying pan was even warm I was running out of the hut to do battle with the first fish that had rocketed the float under. It weighed 3·6kg (8lb) and was followed within a quarter of an hour by a similar fish, and both gave twice the fight normally expected from pike in this water. From then on all I had to do was work my way up or downstream, carefully selecting water where the flow was just above the unflooded normal and was rewarded with jack and small pike up to 3·6kg (8lb).

Then, when I started to use bigger baits, small mackerel and 20cm (8in) rudd, I began catching better pike, the heaviest 6·3kg (14lb) odd, which was very good for a water where a fish of 4·5kg (10lb) had been the previous best. In my opinion it was not the increased bait size – in terms of food – that influenced the larger pike into taking; I am convinced that in the coloured water that I had been fishing those larger baits were more visible and attracted the better fish from farther out, fish able to withstand more in terms of flow strength. Since then I have been convinced that colour, both light and size-wise, is all-important.

Had I not then left my native Sussex and moved to Wales for a few years, my knowledge and experience of fast-water angling would in all probability have remained tied to fishing during and after times of flood. Not that one would really suspect that pike are widespread throughout the Principality. When I arrived in Wales to seek pike fishing I found a near-conspiracy to deny that such fish even existed in its waters. I have seen game fishermen on the Towy gazing at a pike which I had taken from the water mere minutes before with an expression on their faces which suggested that I had brought the fish with me – surely *that* could never have come from one of the fairest and foremost game fisheries in the Principality!

One of the pleasures that I take from this attitude is that piking remains practically virgin because the presence of the species is unknown – or ignored – and every water can be a delight, varying from the large, powerful river to a little bubbling stream where one would expect to find only small, fat trout.

There is a connection, of course, between game fish and pike because trout form a staple diet for pike in those fast waters, leading to big, powerful, well-fed fish, the best fighters in Britain – and I will stand by those words even when considering loch and lake. The pike stocks never seem to diminish in spite of an all-out war by anglers and associations, combined with aid from water authorities. These pike make excellent eating, too, with fine clean flesh, largely free from that freshwater taint and lack of taste that spoils so many of the coarse fish one tries to eat.

In summer, naturally, fishing on most of the fast-water rivers is out of the question, the game fishermen quite rightly want their say and who is to deny them. Then, once the game season closes the pike angler can get cracking, and I have used the word deliberately. There is no other way that I know of in coming to terms with fast-water pike than to fish regardless of the current right out in the middle of the river, among other fish including the game species. That old idea that pike will skulk in quiet corners, avoiding the current and generally behaving in an 'idle' way, is an old wives' tale. These pike were brought up in fast water and have adapted to living in it, and other than those extreme conditions when they must seek shelter or face injury the pike will definitely avoid slow water.

At times of low water you should study the pools first, when the structure of the bottom can be seen. Throughout the length of most runs you will see a strong fold in the floor, an area of deep water usually shelving off steeply to one side or the other. In pools with a rock bed there will be a succession of scour holes and miniature gorges, some very deep indeed, often preceded by a bar or outcrop at the head of the pool which splits the current.

On bends there will be a gradual slope in the bed towards the concave side, a slow taper that leads to where the river bites into the bank as it erodes its path. Even on straight lengths of the river there will seldom be a constant depth, the fast-moving current scouring all kinds of passages out of the bed as softer material becomes worn and eroded leaving banks and boulders under the surface, which in turn help to divert the current towards fresh scouring places. All of those places where the depth varies will hold pike and to get at them you must be prepared to use your angling brains and try to devise tackle that will match the challenge. It is pointless to use the normal pike rod, reel and line to work a bait in these conditions, nor even the usual baits and rigs. With but a slight winter flow the current will take most baits through the water at express speed and they will repeatedly tangle with the bottom and produce constant breaks: of course, some tackle is bound to be lost but with some hard work and sensible balance much can be avoided.

My standard outfit for fishing this kind of river when it becomes winter swollen is light sea fishing tackle. At this point many readers will throw up their hands in horror, but with a sensible balance through rod, line and reel it is possible to cover the water and land fish in a sporting manner, and this is something few fast-water anglers concentrate on nowadays, when the move towards lighter tackle often leads to more lost fish breaking free with hooks in their mouths. I favour a 3·6m (12ft) beachcaster capable of using weights up to 170g (6oz) though it will take slightly more without becoming strained. My reel is a multiplier because it enables me to keep a tighter line control, especially in windy weather, and I seldom drop the line below 8kg (18lb) breaking strain. Alasticum traces, and so on, match this strength.

Fig 4

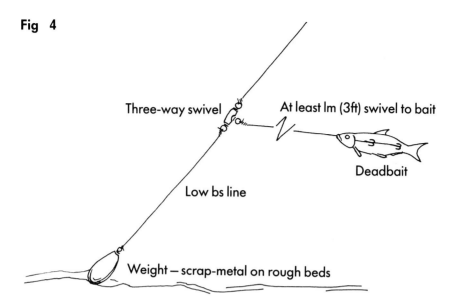

Three-way swivel   At least lm (3ft) swivel to bait

Deadbait

Low bs line

Weight — scrap-metal on rough beds

Floats are not only unnecessary but positively useless in these waters and so for the most part are baits left static over long periods. Fishing here requires a moving bait with the rod always held in the hand; rigs must allow for this mobile kind of tactic and prevent any tangle as far as possible. This immediately rules out all those complex combinations of innumerable swivels, beads, stop shot, trigger mechanisms and all the other refinements that can be used in still or semi-still water fishing.

My basic rig is shown in Fig 4 and I have yet to know one to better it. The line is led down to a three-way swivel, sea-fishing size, and below that a length of line, of finer breaking strain than that used on the reel, connects to the weight. This of course must match the speed and strength of the water, heavy enough to hold the bottom but light enough to be lifted by the rod tip to allow the rig to roll farther downstream when required and keeping the bait on the move.

I often use slab-sided casting sea leads, which are far less likely to snag on the bed than the usual pear-shaped weights that wedge so easily on rock outcrops and sunken debris. From the side-ring on the three-way swivel I secure a metre (3ft) or so of line, the same breaking strain as that used on the reel, to which is attached the trace and hooks.

At this point we should pause and consider baits for this kind of fishing. Anything small will not be seen, and anything too large will simply hamper casting, more especially as the rig I have just described tends to be rather lop-sided. Baitfish of about 22·8cm (9in) are about the right size but if there is a good push of water and it is not too heavily discoloured I may try something bigger depending, of course, on the distance to be cast. The mount I use is one of my standard patterns, the bait fished tail-first, the usual treble at the tail and dorsal fin, the trace then passed under the gill cover and out through the mouth thus making for easy casting with the straight pull and not too many hang-ups in the water. A turn or two of very fine round elastic around the bait's body helps to prolong the time the bait remains on the mounts, the elastic yielding slightly but holding, where thread, fine line or monofilament will cut into the flesh of the bait and eventually break it up.

The whole object of fishing with this rig is to get as long a run for the bait to work through as is possible. Cast the maximum distance upstream, take in slack line while keeping the rod in your hand and the rod-tip up, then let the bait rest for about five minutes at the most. Then raise the rod-tip high taking the hands well above your head if necessary in order to lift the weight off the bottom. The complete rig will then trundle a short distance downstream, when you can drop the rod-tip and allow the weight to sink after which, with a suitable pause, the process can be repeated again and again until the stretch of water (or the angler) is exhausted.

'Exhausted' does not, however, mean that there are no fish in the area, it merely indicates that there is for the present no interest. But this situation can always change and I often think that by resting the stretch for half an hour or so and then repeating the tactic fish can be attracted to the bait even when they are not actively feeding. Sometimes I have worked a bait through a run five times or more during a session before picking up a fish without warning. Under those circumstances that fish has usually been a solitary one and of good weight.

On these waters it has been my experience that there is little in the way of a feeding pattern, time-wise at least. If anything governs feeding it is, I am sure, the colour of the water; gin-clear water brings the 'feast of the passover' and a slight tinge of colour is best. When the water is really dark that old dodge of part-gutting a bait and leaving its stomach open often pays off either through the scent or the sudden attraction of the whole flabby viscera flapping past the pike's eyes, but I am not certain which of these is the deciding factor.

One useful dodge when facing gin-clear water is to run a kited bait. The essential bait is a dead freshwater fish such as a roach or rudd or, best of all, a skimmer bream. The fish is mounted on the rod, reel and trace described above but connects directly to the line through a swivel without any weight other than just sufficient at the bait's nose to ensure that it tips gently down in the water. This can be done by experiment at the water's edge until the right amount is arrived at. The rig is then cast well upstream of the run and the bait allowed to roll and turn freely through the area, line being released from the reel so that a long-trot occurs. The bait will not move at an even depth, but will usually rise and fall and swing towards and away from the banks, generally kiting in a manner that often seems to invoke a strike from any pike in the area. These takes are certainly not the gentle, cross-body grips; the angler sees a heavy swirl followed by an immediate lunge on the line.

The subject of takes is an interesting one. There will often be what I call two bites at the cherry. When the rod is being held one is aware that the bait has been held, then suddenly released after a few seconds or occasionally a little longer. At this point hang in there and don't panic, but lift the rod tip momentarily to pull the bait forward just a metre. In nine cases out of ten you get a definite take straight away.

Through the course of a season there will be occasions when it may be possible to fish by a more regular approach. To illustrate this, I remember a mild, near rain-free October when the river lay docile and I fished at Hay-on-Wye, in Wales. Using livebaits and concentrating on an area of bends and small eddies I caught five good fish using the traditional rods, reels and line, even down to the float that – like it or not – really does add excitement to the sport. Unfortunately such days on the middle and lower stretches of fast, powerful rivers are the exception and not the rule.

The question of livebait is, of course, a sore point where the game angler is concerned, who feels that coarse fish are introduced into water where there are already enough. And the sight of a pike fisherman using live or even dead trout as bait does nothing to lower blood pressure or encourage a friendly relationship with anglers of different persuasions. To be frank I have to admit that I have used both live and dead trout as bait and have found them not to possess any greater attraction than that provided by a good-sized mackerel, roach or rudd. What matters during the winter months is colour and size, while snob value and 'quality fish' do not affect a pike's palate.

Those anglers who spin where it is allowed on game waters usually adopt the standard cast-out-and-retrieve method as used by the game fisherman himself. The spinners are similar too, but heavier, naturally, because of the extra flow during the winter period. This is all fair fishing and good sized pike will be taken. However, many more will be missed, especially where the bottom of a river is uneven. With the traditional method a spinner will pass over the heads of a large number of fish, often well above them. In fact, unless considerable weight is added to the trace above a spinner the push of the current will keep it within about a metre (3ft) of the surface. But it is possible to get a spinner down near the riverbed even on broken ground and the rig and style with which to do it is exactly the same as that recommended for deadbaiting using the beachcaster and paternoster. Instead of using a bait, a spinner is mounted and the procedure for casting, holding while the spinner revolves, then raising the rod-tip and allowing the rig to work downstream, remains the same.

Again, that theory of big-bait-big-attractor does not work in this instance and I have often caught a large pike while using nothing bigger than the largest Mepps bait. These leaf-type spinners are always a good bet; spoons and Tobys don't reach anywhere near their 'working' rate of revolution and this, I am sure, is important, especially when the water is coloured. Soon I am going to try Bombers Bushwacker lures (mentioned in Chapter 3), for I feel that the extra weight, plus two revolving vanes, might well give extra attraction.

I have seen the plug bait worked in the same way by game fishermen on fast water but must admit that I have never used it in this mode because it does not seem the right thing to do: a plug is designed to swoop, swing and move constantly and it must lose some of its attraction if it is tethered or anchored. By using a base anchor it must also follow that the depth at which the lure will work must remain constant. Lowering the rod-tip or raising it will merely alter the depth of retrieve momentarily. The only method available is to vary the length of line between the bottom of the three-way swivel and the weight itself at intervals until a taking depth is found, and this can be a nuisance. More often than not I allow about a metre (3ft) from the lead to the swivel when deadbaiting or spinning, but habit is the most blind and damning thing in fishing and I know that I must experiment more with the tethered spinner and plug by fishing it at varying depths.

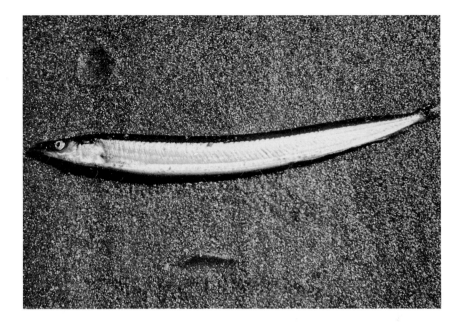

13 *A fine bait: the sandeel, mounted on a light rig and fished along the stream in fast water, takes fish time and time again. It is effective when other, more cumbersome whole dead-fish baits fail to attract pike*

The higher one travels upstream into the headwaters the finer one's tackle can become, largely because there is no need for long casts; and smaller baits do not need strong tackle. There will, too, be little occasion for using a float and the scaled-down flowing paternoster works equally well upstream as on the downstream beats. One other rig works like a dream on the smaller fast waters. It is the drop sprat, mounted as explained in Chapter 5, and it must be fished into exact places rather than allowed to roam and drift at random. A precision cast is made followed by two or three lifts of the rod-tip and if there is a pike there the chances are that it will take your offering immediately.

There is one rig and bait that I discovered by accident and I have kept it to myself until now. It is the sandeel (Photograph 13). Its discovery came by accident some four years ago when I was worming for sewin on a small Welsh river. Feeling a take, I struck and instead of the anticipated seatrout there was a bootlace eel, already tying itself into a knot as it was coming to the surface – then suddenly it was in the jaws of a sizeable pike. Of course, the line snapped and it was gone.

My obvious thought after the pike had departed was that here was a food supply never before thought about by anglers, but one which pike must take during those times of the year when eels are active. I pondered on how big the eels could be that pike fed on, but commonsense dictated that they would not be overlarge. Unfortunately there was no way I could see how to catch small live eels, keeping them alive and then using them as bait. And added to that the thought of livebaiting with an eel with any chance of success was beyond my imagination.

It was during a bass-fishing outing when I thought of using sandeels and I bought a dozen to try them out. They were kept frozen until I required them for a trip to a small local stream, fishing with a small, slim coarse-fishing float in conjunction with spinning tackle that terminated in a single hook, mounted to fine Alasticum, liphooked through the mouth of the sandeel. I had three takes which left the eel chopped short just behind the head, so some hasty thinking resulted in amendments to the method of mounting the bait. Instead of a lip-mount, the hook was taken into the mouth, down through and out of the bottom of the jaw and then led along to the mid-section where it was skin-nicked, leaving the point of the barb exposed (see Fig 5). After that there was little trouble from the point of view of hooking. Pike took the bait readily and were brought to the bank, but so did many other coarse species. Chub were the problem on Welsh waters, and in England, where I have used the method successfully, perch have been a nuisance. Game fish, of course, are always attracted to the wriggling sandeel, especially the lone cannibal trout.

Though I dislike legering for pike I must admit that the sandeel does work well with this method, but using the flowing rig described in Chapter 7 with one small modification. Because the bait is so small the current will not feed it freely through the eye of the plastic ring. A

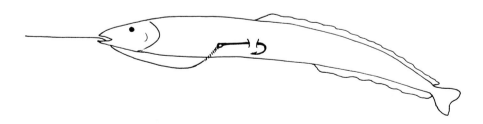

Fig 5

14 *Sandeels are a good freshwater bait but difficult to obtain in any numbers. These are being kept alive by a professional sea fisherman for use as bass baits. For piking they must be frozen immediately after being individually wrapped*

simple compromise is a torpedo-shaped bubblefloat, part filled with water, and attached on the bait side of the ring, which runs easily on the current and with some judicious holding back from the angler will stream the bait nicely behind it.

The big problem remains, however: how to obtain sufficient sandeels. The market does offer some jars of very well-preserved baits, but of necessity they are small. It is far better to try to make the acquaintance of one of the professional fishermen on the coast (I have one in Poole, Dorset) where they net at regular intervals and often sell at the quayside. The sandeels can be freeze-dried in paper and sealed in plastic the same as for ordinary deadbaits and they are perfect when required.

I am considering the possibility of an artificial sandeel, not one of the plastic models which do work, though not quite as effectively as the real thing, but one tied from a feather or similar free-moving material that will really wriggle and trail when retrieved. The difficulty will be in finding the right feather or material.

The matter of attaching a sandeel to the treble of a spinner has already been mentioned and it certainly seems to supply the lure with a little something extra in attraction. In headwaters and the upper reaches of fast-flowing rivers sandeels do not last long and I tend to keep them for slower waters, only because the supply of baits is always hard to maintain. But in those waters there never seems any difficulty in inducing pike to take a spinner of any kind, the only problem being one of losing tackle on the shallow, rough bottoms that seem to reach up and grab at the lure as it swings past.

When your tackle is caught up and snagged remember that it is quite senseless in straining the rod, line and reel mechanism in trying to free it. Lay the rod down, wind a few coils of line round your forearm *over the sleeve of your jacket* and ease the line back. It often frees without undue strain but when it is recovered do not fail to examine knots, hooks (in case they may have straightened) and the points for blunting. If you fail to make these checks don't complain if the next fish you hook gets away and is lost.

It is the smaller, fast waters where the plug comes into its own. The plugs that float, with a small vane that induces a shallow, controlled dive are excellent and can be worked into the most awkward places following a little prior thought on exactly how the retrieve will be made. Simply retrieving blindly when plug fishing can become an expensive exercise when you have to replace costly plugs.

It is not possible to consider fast-water fishing without mentioning weirpools. Next to the accumulation of spinners and plugs, weirpools are probably the biggest drug to which the angler is exposed. Like it or not, we find the feet automatically heading towards the roar of tumbling water and once in its presence it is near-impossible not to avoid making a few casts, even spending the whole day fishing the pool below the open gates. The sound and movement of the water seems to build up an expectation in the angler: something *surely* must happen at any moment!

And one is seldom disappointed with a day's weirpool fishing. During the early season, even on the hottest of days, a pike will often oblige even though it is out of condition and well below the weight it should be. The strength of the current, too, will add its pull to the slowest fish.

There is no straightforward method or even a clearly defined approach to fishing in the area of a weir. Every time the gates are adjusted, each time there is a push of water downstream from heavy rain the conditions will change. Often, each day that you fish during a winter of hard weather you will find that the bed of the pool will have altered its shape and that the current will be running in another place to that which existed when you fished it last. The main flume of water pushing downstream will have scoured a deep channel, throwing gravel to each side and depositing a wide bar of debris and shingle at the end of the pool where the current slackens and allows water-borne objects to sink. As various gates are opened and closed some of the deep channels may not receive their usual push of water, depending of course on the size of the weir, and the deeper water, at the bar end, is one good place to seek a pike.

The areas round the bank edges are always good holds and that means the bank at your feet, not the one across on the other side of the pool. This being the case it needs a cautious and low approach to the water's edge followed by some sensible casting and working of the bait if a nearby fish is not to be frightened out of the area.

In winter, I have found the best weir fishing to be well below the pool itself, under the banks past which the stream pushes and where the earth will have subsided or been undercut. Here, the current will have made a succession of holes that become pike holds. It is pleasant fishing too. The bait can be float-fished, cast slightly into the stream, the rod in the hand and the line held back so that the float swings in and is then allowed to trundle slowly downstream, being checked at each likely-looking spot. Easier still is paternoster fishing, which necessitates the angler keeping well away from the water's edge and this will be found the most successful rig when the current is running at any strength. For the deeper holes and runs out from the banks one can leger with a running trace that allows a deadbait to move about 'searching' for fish. This is a most telling style and must appear extremely natural to a hungry pike, which sees a dead fish rolling over and over in the current. It probably accounts for the firmness of a take when this rig is employed.

For me, the pleasure in fishing a weirpool is in the plug and spinner, searching the side of the main run, especially during the summer months, working up under the apron of the weir where the fish will lie sheltered from extreme water pressure and confident of plenty of food in the form of the small fry that are always superabundant there. It is also a productive area in the poorer weather when cold has forced many fish into a torpor and general disinterestedness.

The best place for plug fishing is the tail of the weir. Here, the adaptability of the plug comes into its own in the uneven bed where there is often massive debris, even whole trees and branches can be found part buried. However, these barriers are themselves holds for fish and woe betide the angler who does not act decisively at the moment of hooking in the proximity of this kind of obstruction for it takes but seconds for a struggling pike to tie and knot the line round some underwater snag. But tackle losses are inevitable at times when one is fishing for pike in fast water. It takes just a little commonsense to realise that the risk may well justify the loss and you must ensure that a line break or lost fish will not be brought about by your lack of imagination and observation.

5
Slow Waters

Slow waters are my preference possibly because I am a southerner, born in a part of the country where lush meadows and meandering rivers mean slow, deliberate fishing styles. More practically, my love of fishing stems from the thousands of hours I have spent piking on the Thames, due in no small measure to one Isambard Brunel, who sited his Great Western Railway stations at pike-fishing centres along that river. The good thing about slow-water fishing is its comfort, a strange word to associate with pike fishing which is practised in the hardest of weather and during the most open and exposed months of the year. But there is a particular comfort associated with slow rivers, not simply from the fishing but from the water, down to the trees and bushes lining the banks, the cattle grazing in the meadow, even human habitation, rarely far away. Even the fishing is comfortable, with pike in plenty spread along the watercourse. There is no need to walk long distances or to make long casts to catch them and the angler can often bank half-a-dozen during an outing, but although there are plenty of pike they are usually small ones.

Angling records I have kept over many years do not show many slow-waters that support pike weighing 13·6kg (30lb) or over and my experience and that of other pike anglers is that the better pike from average waters fluctuate between 4·5 and 9kg (10 and 20lb), those over 9kg (20lb) being notable fish that might turn up once or twice in several seasons. The reason for the small average size of these pike is due very probably to the native stock of the waters. A pike from a fast water will be long and lean, its weight, which can be quite considerable, is carried the length of the body and not concentrated at the shoulders or belly. This is especially so on game fishing rivers. The pike there are built to fight the stream, chasing food fish and coping with extreme conditions such as floods and fluctuating water levels.

On the other hand, the slow-water pike that are so numerous amount to nothing much in terms of weight. They will be short, rotund fish that cannot add weight to a body length that is not there. Their lifestyle is opposite to that of the fast-water pike; they never need fight for survival, food will come to them as they lie in the safety of their holts. In my opinion few slow-water pike ever travel very far up or downstream away from their original territory through the course of their lives. But though the pike are small, the surrounding environments of the Thames waters they inhabit are among the prettiest. Fascinating pike fishing can be had in the river in the area of Hartslock Wood, above Pangbourne, Poplar Island and Appletree Eyot at Tilehurst, and the Henley bankside with its locks, weirs and downstream islands. All these places were – and in some cases still are – within walking distance of a railway station and before our affluent car-owning society came into being the train was the only means of transport to the water at weekends.

In the early 1950s each Thames fishing station had its own pike fishermen and a cameraderie existed among them. Most had their nicknames, and I remember 'Spinning Jack' and 'The Trout', so called from his habit of killing and keeping all Thames trout he caught whether or not they were taken out of season. This was just after World War II when trout were more numerous in the Thames than they are today. In the winter the local railway stations would disgorge a number of these stalwarts, all muffled up in a great show of ex-Service clothing. A forest of rods heralded their approach, livebait kettles slopping water with every step. A float-fished livebait was the only piking method then.

In that period I spent ten years regularly pike-fishing the Thames and I recall only three or four anglers who paternostered or legered. Even fewer resorted to spinning in spite of the gradual availability of fixed-spool reels that made casting much easier than with the centre-pin. I once watched an angler spinning for pike at Pangbourne weirpool with a tubular steel rod and an American multiplier. Every slack and run was searched and he landed four pike on a Colorado spoon that twinkled like a jewel as it turned in the water. Then I found that he was a Thames trout angler keeping his casting technique sharp during the close game season. But any mention of Pangbourne recalls another never-to-be-forgotten character known as the 'Dude'. He arrived every Saturday morning, dressed to the nines and carrying a small tackle holdall and neat rod bag. On arrival at the waterside he would put on galoshes and make his way carefully to the nearest swim. First he caught some livebait, then he put up a pike rig. He never sat down, never moved to another swim and I never saw him catch a pike. Then one day the mystery was solved. We found that his wife, of whom he was terrified, thought fishing was cruel and had banned him from the sport. So on Saturday mornings he dressed as if he was going to a job in Town, collected his tackle from a pal and went fishing.

But I must admit that the early years I spent fishing the Thames were mostly wasted. The river was a drug, it stopped me thinking and working out new tactics, new tackle rigs. I got into a rut with the same train, the same anglers, the same swims week after week. My livebait was the same, my tackle was the traditional set-up, a *Fishing Gazette* float and Jardine snap tackle. I never attempted to spin although I practised it on other waters. They were happy times but the slow and easy-going atmosphere became an opiate and I needed to be jolted out of the reverie and the jolt came in the form of a boat.

The boat I bought was nothing special, 2·4m (8ft) of marine ply glued, screwed and varnished, and stored in a friend's garden that backed onto the Thames. It had no engine and I used to strain my arms trying to row against the stream to prime pike-fishing spots. Then I discovered that my low-level approach across the water, my ability to move freely up and down-stream to chart new places on wide stretches of river where so far no baits had been cast, allowed me to use my imagination as to what was going on beneath the surface. This changed my whole approach to pike fishing. At this time, too, a revolution took place in piking. Deadbaits became the rage, fixed-spool reels and lightweight but strong hollow glass-fibre rods made casting a pleasure, avoiding the double ruptures experienced by anglers when using the heavy wood and brass of the old tackles.

Above all, I found another piece of equipment that was as essential as sharp hooks — an old, glass aquarium. I did not fill it full of water and introduce goldfish, but took it with me on my boat fishing trips, where, when pushed into the surface of the water, it cut out refraction and enabled me to see into all those hot spots that held fish and those places I had thought barren. To my surprise those great expanses of lilies on the downstream side of islands, never fished in the summer, were full of pike. And in winter when I thought that the pike had left to seek shelter and relative comfort after the lilies had died back, there the fish still were, hugging the bottom and blending among the huge rhizomes twisting and curling above the riverbed.

All those hot spots held good fish and I also found that there were more pike under the bank from where one was fishing than were out in midstream. It seems that pike are frightened away from the water in front of anglers, unless these are of the lone-wolf kind who take their fishing seriously and make sure that the foreground is not disturbed by the silhouette of an angler. So instead of avoiding losing tackle in those places where there were snags I began working my deadbaits into those very unlikely spots. It immediately revolutionised my ordinary float-fished live or deadbaiting methods. Until then my deadbaiting had been with herring, fished head-first because that was the dictum of the time, based on the premise that pike must have the bait down to the throat before they could be hooked. But any attempt to fish with a herring mounted in that way among the lilies or reedbeds led to immediate disaster. Weed always becomes wedged between the trace and the tail of the fish, forcing the hooks away from the body as the bait is retrieved. An improvement is obtained by tying the trace at the tail, but it is not a cure because the soft flesh of the herring soon gives way at the knot, cutting the tail free and wrenching hooks out of the body.

A better way, I discovered, was by mounting the herring the other way round, with the end treble at the tail, one at the dorsal fin (in the manner of the Jardine snap tackle), then taking the trace through the gill slit and out through the mouth before attaching it with a link swivel to the line (Fig 6). This mounting streamlined the bait so that without a float or any weight it could be worked into places where before I would not have considered it worthwhile. And even if the tackle did become snagged I just had to row into the area and retrieve

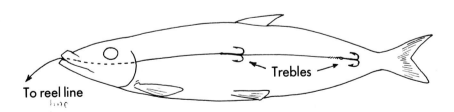

To reel line

Trebles

Fig 6

it, saving wear and tear and, more important, strain. Few anglers seem to consider the importance of strain on their tackle, but heaving and tugging to free a snagged hook puts an enormous strain on the line and packs it fiercely onto the spool, causing jams and breaks and exerting enormous compression strains. The pick-up arm on a fixed spool suffers particularly, and the line itself can lose 20 per cent of its strength. It is better to cut the line and accept losses when there is no hope of getting out of a snag. If your tackle is weakened at some place it is there that it will break when you are playing a good fish.

My summer piking out in the boat and among the weeds gave me some excellent fish. I had one pike of 7·7kg (17lb) and two of 6·8kg (15lb) taken in two days. However I was far from satisfied with herring as a summer bait and soon turned to mackerel. It might be thought that this decision took me a long while, but behind it lay some careful reasoning. Most mackerel are too big to be used as summer pike baits and a half-mackerel trimmed and mounted with the cut end first, the shape of plummet, would seem to be the natural conclusion. But it isn't. While this bait is readily accepted by winter pike – the oil slick oozing from the mackerel helps to draw the pike near – summer fish are not over-attracted by something that has been hacked about. I experimented by casting out a whole herring, followed by half a mackerel, placing them side by side and then with the aid of my glass aquarium watching them on the bottom. I saw that the whole fish stood out clearly but the half mackerel sank and blended into the background of weeds until it was all but invisible. Unless attracted by scent, the pike would not see the smaller bait.

Then a sea-fishing pal provided the solution. Early in the season young mackerel – the locals call them 'Joeys' – are available inshore. These fish are not sent to market even though they are the same size as the average herring. They made absolutely ideal baits and now I make a couple of trips to the coast every year to stock my freezer with them. Now, 'Joey' mackerel are my standard bait and when they are used in place of the soft-fleshed herring my baiting-up time is halved – which increases the number of pike I catch. So now even in winter I avoid a cut bait whenever possible, and am convinced that a whole bait is preferable.

That summer pike fishing was good, but the winter sport exceeded it by a considerable margin. My usual approach was to row slowly upstream of the area to be fished and then, using a running float stopped with a knot and bead plus a small mackerel injected with the smallest amount of air that would cause it to float just off the bottom, start at the end of a long stretch and search the water through by long trotting. With 18m (20yd) or more of line out it was a simple matter to quietly lift the anchor of the boat and slowly drift downstream, anchoring again and allowing the bait to work farther ahead. Quiet, sure, deadly and fascinating in early autumn and winter, before weather and rain gave too much flow on the water. Often in clear water one could see the turn of a pike that moved out to seize the bait, and then one could watch the fish from the time the strike had been made through to the actual landing.

Few anglers are aware of the fight that a pike puts up when it is hooked. The angler is aware of the strain, pull and weight on a rod once the hooks are in, but most anglers are completely unaware of the enormous struggle that takes place when we cannot see what is happening. I have seen fish, once the hooks were driven home, turn complete somersaults and others that have done a violent figure of eight spin. The amount of upwards movement and diving is always completely out of proportion to the play experienced at the rod handle. The instinct possessed by fish in their ability to manoeuvre into fast currents, weedbeds or similar obstructions is uncanny even if in the end they fail to regain their freedom.

In my boat I often worked a mile or more fishing in this fashion, but the sport always came to a stop when heavy water came into the river. Then, colour and current demanded a different approach. Not all my summer observations of hot-spots centred on areas of weed and I had been careful to learn the contours of the river bed both in the main channel and on the bends, especially against the non-towpath side of the river where there was a great deal of private land with unfished water in front of it. Had I assumed the bed of the Thames to be a fascinating panorama of holes, gullies, plateaux and underwater hillocks, I was in for a bitter disappointment. For the greater part, especially in the navigational channel, the river was gently curved towards the centre line between the banks and lay entirely clear of blemishes which one would imagine that fish preferred to hide in. Where there was a crater or hole it invariably seemed to have been caused by debris, large tree branches and such like, swept down during

15 *The contents of the author's summer pike-fishing box. Deadbait rigs, poppers and jigs that pack into small spaces are essential if the best of summer sport is to be experienced*

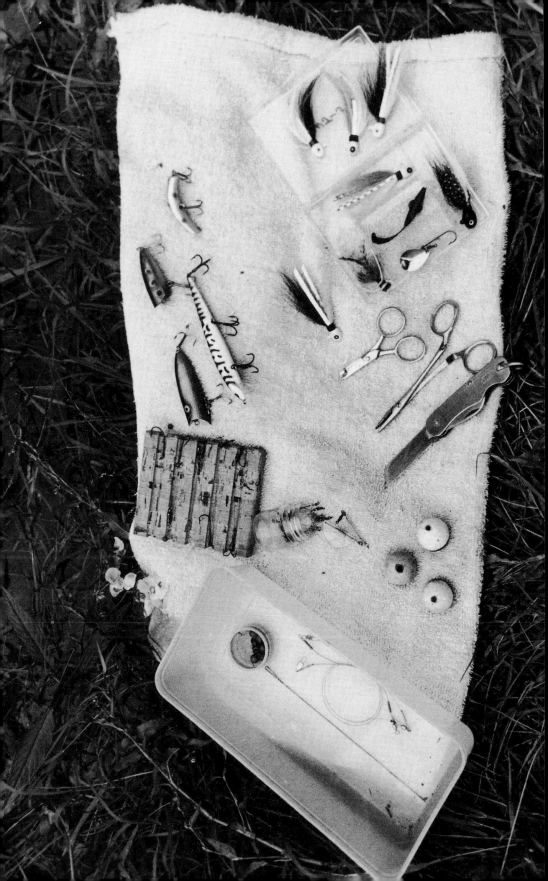

floods and trapped on the bottom to become a scouring point or silt trap.

One very significant thing, and an important lesson too, was that the colour of the riverbed always varied dramatically even over short distances: and it was the colour of the riverbed that governed to a large extent where the pike would lie in the winter. Providing there was some good, thick, black or very dark brown mud or silt, even stones or dark shingle, even in comparatively small areas, half a dozen or more pike would congregate there. It seemed that they tended to lie just to the edges of the dark areas, avoiding the centres. My tentative theory about this is that their prey would be seen in silhouette, lit by reflection from the light gravel outside the dark area, while the pike remain hidden.

When I became aware of this I had some success with a large legered deadbait dropped in the area on the fringes of the dark spots. But remembering the numbers of pike I had observed it became clear that I was not catching as many as I should have done. There were two reasons for this. The first was that the bait retrieved between casts would often come back with a covering of weed and silt round the trace, enough to hide the deadbait. From my observations when using the aquarium I saw that it was caused by 'snubbing', movements of the current tugging at the anchored bait lying on top of the bed, working against it so that it gradually received a covering. So I adapted an item of sea anglers' rig, a piece of polyurethane or half a cork mounted just behind the swivel between trace and line, which lifted the head of the bait slightly off the riverbed. It worked but was clumsy and looked it. I have an intense dislike of clumsiness in anything to do with fishing regardless of the species.

The second and better step to catching more of the pike I knew to be there was to abandon legering altogether and concentrate on the paternoster. But I do not like using the method in slow waters and only tolerate it when I have to. Again, from watching what was happening underwater I could see that twist and tangle often occurred between bait and line above the anchoring weight. So I tried all kinds of tricks and discussed the problem with other anglers, but in the end arrived at

One cannot imagine fish being handled like this during today's angling attitudes – but it happened during a day spent on a pike cull where fish were being taken, but were to be destroyed. Perhaps the knowledge that there was no future for the fish caused the angler to pose like this. Certainly it cannot be allowed to continue, and pike culls that encourage this behaviour must, themselves, be culled

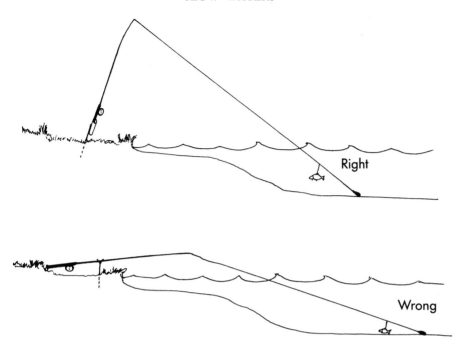

Fig 7

the method I use today and which is described in Chapter 4, Fig 4. But instead of a long, flowing trace between bait and swivel I keep to a mere 45 cm (18 in) or so. In slow water I rarely use a float, it simply becomes a nuisance either by lying flat on the surface or pulling just beneath it if I have misjudged the depth where I am fishing.

Paternostering from a boat is the opposite to that method described in an earlier chapter. Beginning at the upstream end of a stretch I anchor and then cast *upstream*, holding the rod high or supporting it against a thwart so that the rod tip is as near the vertical as possible. By doing this I keep the bait where it should be, just off the bottom. If the rod is laid down or allowed to dip at the tip, this allows the bait to drop to the river bed as when legering and that is not paternostering. Once a cast has been made the bait can be slowly worked back to the boat two or three yards at a time, then the boat allowed to drop downstream so

Typical gravel-pit pike. This pit has settled for some sixteen years or more and now supports a good head of fish up to 11·3 kg (25 lb) or so. The constant hill and underwater valley bed of the pit needs careful study if best results are to be obtained

that all the water is covered without recapping. One can fish 183m (200yd) at a time with a single cast, unless of course a pike takes the bait before the area is fished out. No matter how very tantalizing it is, do not keep reeling in and casting back to 'interesting' spots either side of the boat. You must know the riverbed and the course along which you are going to fish, so fish it out. If necessary go back to fish it again with the boat on another course to take in those other areas.

Naturally there will be areas that need special attention, invariably the deeper stretches where there is a shoal-off at a bend; or round some of those private boat creeks that back onto the river from large houses. I cast over those areas and bring the paternoster back slowly to the centre spot, taking care to use just enough weight to hold bottom. Many anglers do not understand the connection between weight and paternostering. They attach a lead to the bottom of the rig and leave it there, never allowing for current, clarity of the water or the disturbance that can be caused by too heavy a weight. The smallest weight possible is essential and where there is a chance of snagging I usually use a 'rotten bottom' – a disposable weight such as an engine nut tied to inferior nylon. If the weight snags the weak nylon will break and I will avoid losing useful terminal tackle. Large nuts, too, tend not to become entangled with the meshes of a landing net in the way that pear-shaped leads do, sometimes taking longer to work clear than unhooking the fish does.

I began plug fishing and spinning in stillwater, but it was river fishing that encouraged me to develop the art, for it is a skill and not a game of chance. It is probably due to the size of the Thames that I started to use large lures and stopped worrying about the splash that occurs when they enter the water; many anglers have this concern. But then I realised that on big expanses of water the splash could well be an attraction in itself.

My experience in fishing with artificial lures has been long and I have experimented with every pattern available on a variety of slow waters. It has led me to realise that there is nothing to beat the simple, large silver or silver and copper spoon of one form or another. It is successful because it can be maintained at a constant depth and will not ride to the surface when pressure is increased on it, a problem with many of the modern spinners. Leaf spinners are especially prone to this upward creep and one can be fishing assuming that the lure is working the depths when it is in fact travelling just below the surface. One of the difficulties of spinning from a boat is that the bait is usually where you do not want it to be – well off the bottom. A normal cast toward the bank from a boat in mid-stream needs to be retrieved quickly because the lack of depth means the lure will snag on the bottom, but it can also drag the lure straight out of vision range of a pike lying close by. As the retrieve continues back towards the boat the lure is pulled into the upper layers well away from the riverbed where the best fish are likely to be, often lying beneath the boat. It is no cure to slow the retrieve down, for when you can reach the speed at which the spinner ceases to turn you will be wasting your time.

The alternative is to make long casts immediately downstream from the boat and retrieve the spinner, starting as close to the bank as possible and working outwards in strips towards mid-stream. But I have not had much success with the spinner cast and worked straight up or down a river. There is a solution to this, however. One must spin, or wobble, a deadbait at about 1 knot, giving it plenty of time to sink and hold to the bottom.

This needs strict discipline in the rate of retrieve. The matter of retrieving when spinning is well worth some thought. If you have never considered it, make a point of taking casual observation the next time you are on the bankside. On a cold day watch somebody spinning. He will begin by making careful casts, allowing time for the bait to sink, then retrieving with slow, deliberate turns of the reel handle. If the angler finds a fish all will be well and his disciplined spinning will continue. But if he misses out within an hour several things will happen. First, the retrieve rate will increase, which leads to more casts being made with less attention given to each one. Next, the retrieve will commence as soon as the spinner hits the water: the angler is imagining that if he works harder he will find success. Actually, he will have defeated the object of the exercise because no pike will show interest in a ballistic missile propelled across its vision.

Now to discuss spun or wobbled deadbaits. The slow style on big rivers is not suitable for dead sea fish. Roach or rudd are preferable, rudd certainly so, between 15·2–20·3cm (6–8in) and I am careful when packing them for the freezer to clean them externally and make sure they are laid out straight. If any wobble is required this can be induced by the way the bait is mounted on the trace, but a straight fish will snake and turn in the water very enticingly if left to work with the current and without interference from the angler determined to force the bait to adopt unnatural contours. Mounting deadbaits for this kind of fishing can be difficult, but I use what I call the 'shirt-button' method. Using a baiting needle I thread a shirt-button onto a trace of about 25·4cm (10in), running it down to a single treble whipped onto the opposite end. The needle is then threaded vent-to-mouth or vent to just behind the gill, depending on how much swerve I want to put into it during the retrieve. This is fastened to the main line by a link swivel (see Fig 8). It is a simple matter, taking a few minutes to complete. The advantage of that shirt-button is that it prevents the treble from being pulled into the body of the bait and the trace is not going to snag or cut into the fish either. A very useful ploy is to use a barleycorn lead slid down the trace into the mouth of the bait, and held in place by tying the mouth closed with silk thread, as an extra weight when water conditions are heavy.

This is an extra bit of fussiness and since I am always trying to avoid 'tackle tinkering' I use it only when it is necessary to get the bait down onto or just off the bottom. The subject of wobbled deadbaits cannot be left without mentioning baitfish other than roach or rudd. The obvious species for use as a bait in any style would be trout, but not in my experience as a deadbait. Somehow I find that they do not have that essential movement or visual attraction to make a successful wobbler bait. Small, hand-sized bream can be very good baits, their flat bodies really do turn and tumble when being retrieved. But I have never caught them in sufficient numbers to freeze and they would take up a lot of room too, no matter how tightly packed they were.

Let us finish with big, slow waters and discuss those many small waters of which there are far more, right down to tiny streams that are feeders for larger ones. All these can supply sport as fine as that found on the larger and wider expanses. I never cease to be amazed at the size and quality of fish that can be taken from the smaller waters and it is a style of fishing that has great appeal to me. The rewards, however, are

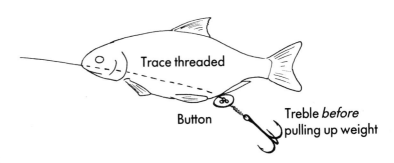

Trace threaded

Button

Treble *before* pulling up weight

Fig 8

strictly in keeping with the size of stream being fished; nobody but a fool would expect to find fish in the 9kg (20lb) range in a water where the food supply, cover and room are not sufficient to enable large fish to develop. However, in many small waters pike can find the shelter they need and this is not just by lying among weedbeds. They will be found where the bank is undercut, among tree roots, and even alongside and partly hidden by debris of all kinds, all this in water sometimes as shallow as 0·2m (2ft). The clue to fishing these places is to get the bait into all the unlikely spots; treat every inch of the stream as if it is bound to hold fish and forget the normal, big-water tactic of reading the water and then concentrating on the selected, obvious areas.

My preference for small-water pike fishing is such that I regularly use the small spinning rod described in Chapter 3. The reel is still the ABU closed-face model, deliberately chosen in spite of many theoretical problems of line-feed, to remove some of the risk of tangling with bankside herbage, and there is always plenty of that no matter where one is fishing. I keep to line of 2·2kg (5lb) and the traces, floats, swivels, anti-kinks and so on are all to match. My deadbait for slow waters is invariably sprats and the rig involves one treble only, mounted at the eye of the fish with the trace tied to the tail to hold it parallel. With it, one can very nearly swim the stream in the knowledge that in the shallow water the bait will be visible for most of its journey downstream. Those places where there is any real depth can be usually covered by using a paternoster. 'Usually' because there will be good places that are so covered by bankside vegetation the year round that it is impossible to get a bait in there. The temptation is to cut out and clear a space to make the water available, but resist that feeling for all you will do is ruin the place. You may take a pike from it immediately but when you return another day all you will catch there will be jack pike. Clearing thick vegetation is not worth the effort, for large pike are wary of open areas and avoid them.

In slow waters where casting requires rifle-sharp accuracy I have found nothing to beat the drop-tackle. Photograph 16 shows this rig, which is made quickly and cheaply by using a barleycorn lead glued with Araldite onto a short length of copper wire to one end of which an eye has been turned. This supports the trace with its single treble and single hook plus at the line end a link swivel. The whole thing is designed to take a sprat although, naturally, one can use the rig in geared-up form for any size of deadbait.

Mounting the bait is easy, the lead and wire go into the mouth of the sprat and a turn of silk holds it in place. Use embroidery silk, it is fine enough not to be too apparent, easy to tie and holds without slipping during tying. For some traditional reason I use red silk, but I have no reason to believe that pike would respond differently to another colour. The hooks are mounted as shown Photograph 16 and another turn of silk stops bait and tail hook from coming apart. With a light rod, fine line and without a float the bait can be cast headfirst straight into odd corners and holes where it would be difficult to project the normal rig.

The bait should be allowed to sink to the bottom then retrieved by the sink-and-draw style, giving it plenty of time to peak and tumble, making it one of the deadliest methods, the most important thing being that the retrieve must be unhurried. A feeding pike usually takes when the bait has been lifted, then allowed to sink, which often causes it to loop in the water and revolve once or twice. It is an action that a feeding pike of any size cannot resist and I have had double-figure fish lunging so hard at the sprat that they have been hooked without the need for a strike. A point that I have observed while fishing small waters is that there is no need to spend time calculating the exact moment when a strike should be made. It is as if the pike are so intent on seizing the bait that the pouch and swallow are simultaneous. Perhaps a comparatively meagre food supply is at the root of it, or the smallness of the water indicates that the next pike is not far away and is ready to lunge at what is hesitated over. But whatever the reason, striking is easy on small waters and not having to perform deep surgery to recover tackle from badly hooked fish is yet another reason for my liking of these waters.

Jigs and poppers are described in Chapter 3, but they must be mentioned briefly here. On some small, deep waters these lures can be irresistible to pike, but not by any means on all slow streams. Inexplicably, on some streams jigs and poppers actually frighten pike away as soon as they are used, no matter how carefully they are cast or worked. And on those waters where they succeed in attracting pike they evoke immediate action, especially in the summer, a time when pike do seem more adventurous in their feeding habits. Some of the jigs and poppers I use are shown in Photograph 15 together with the other pike gear for small waters, seen already packed in the polythene box in the background. With that tackle, plus a bag of sprats, or some means of catching suitable baits, I can use half-a-dozen fishing styles through

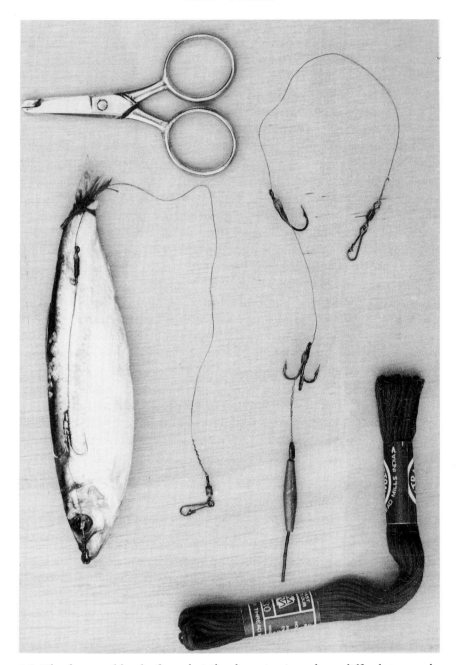

16 *The drop-tackle, the finest bait for dropping into those difficult-to-reach, dark corners. Cheap to make and easy to use it can be fished in places where other rigs are difficult to cast into*

the season, one of which will prove the method for the day summer or winter. Many small waters become unfishable in the winter either because they overflow or run so fast that a bait is unmanageable in the water pressure. But not always – there are times when the smaller water scores over its larger relatives.

On one occasion the stream I was fishing went wild. It was a muggy February day of poor lighting. I began using a float-fished deadbait sprat which as it hit the water charged away into the depths. The pike that took it weighed 2·7kg (6lb), not big but a start. After rebaiting I cast into the same spot and within minutes a second fish, the same weight as the first, was hooked, brought to the bank and released as quickly as possible. From then on I caught pike consistently all day. Twice I had pike on part of a sprat, once when I let the bait drop into the water at my feet as I reached for a sandwich. No matter how badly I cast, how indifferently I approached the water or how clumsy my playing of a fish was, there was always another pike in the queue waiting to be caught and in the four hours I fished there I took fourteen pike for ten sprats. The best fish was 8·3kg (18½lb) and it fell to a mangled sprat backbone and a couple of tatty fins on a well-worn rig. With no baits left I took to using a spoon and caught three more pike under 1·8kg (4lb) until darkness put an end to the day. It never happened again. What caused that remarkable event? I believe that heavy rain had caused serious flooding on the main river but had left the small stream untouched. Erosion of a bank had created water that was as thick as soup, turning the main river's current wild and savage and which must have made my small stream a haven of peace. The pike went to lie there until the river calmed down and I was on hand to take advantage of the situation.

6
Stillwaters

There is no doubt that stillwaters are the highlight in every pike angler's list of fisheries. Vast lochs, lakes in the grounds of stately homes, castle moats, gravelpits, meres, broads – every one of them is capable of firing the imagination. Regardless of whether a pike has ever been caught from the water or even without ever giving serious thought as to whether the water would be capable of supporting the species, let alone a specimen fish, the sight of a still expanse of water will raise the blood pressure to unprecedented heights – and should there not be the remotest chance that permission will ever be granted to fish, then the supreme accolade of longing is reached, it is obvious of course that the water *must* hold big pike.

Pike angling in the light of history has certainly given every cause for hope, and grand fish from places with exciting names live through to the world of today. To read Jardine, Bickerdyke and Trent Otter, to name but a few, is to pump up the blood pressure and escape from the overfished waters of today, and also to give hope for the future.

I must be honest and state that this chapter was nearly entitled 'Deadwaters', which seemed somehow to emphasise the gauntness of those areas with which we associate monster pike. But a few moments thought brought to mind several waters where there is occasional movement, in particular the vast network of canals that span the countryside and where there is a current of some weak fashion albeit during the summer months only. And some of those canals hold excellent fish even though record breakers may be absent, allowing the fishermen to combine the best of slow- and stillwater tactics. I especially recall watching an angler fishing the Regent's Park Canal fighting a pike of 8kg (18lb) which he had hooked. Talk about legwork – he scuttled up and down the towpath like an ageing Sebastian Coe, eventually landing the fish with the help of a passing bargee.

The vast majority of pikemen go for stillwaters above all others and much as the slow-flowing Thames became a drug to me in my early career so stillwaters rapidly extend a similar influence on many of those that fish them. Within a short space of time habit will become set and a high proportion of anglers will occupy the same corner or length of bank for season after season. As they age and spread then so often will be the mountain of tackle and accessories which they bring, whether it is just in case it may be needed, or to promote personal comfort.

If there is any trend towards the angler seeking an improvement in efficiency then it will often show with an increase in the number of rods that are set out. The sight of one angler with six or more rods set up along a section of bank is neither unusual nor, in the majority of cases, more productive of fish either in numbers or weight.

Mind you, I have seen some opposite tactics tried. They are best described in the antics of 'Long John Silver', a relatively young pikeman who haunted the Lee Valley gravelpit system for several years. His nickname came from the enormous bundle of sea-fishing tackle, including beachcasting rods and reels, with line to match, which he carried and used on some of the larger waters which I frequented. His object was to get a bait where no bait had ever been fished before and I *mean* bait. I've seen him punching a 35·5cm (14in) mackerel some 73m (80yd) or more from the bank with a splash-down that would have equalled anything that Cape Canaveral has to offer.

He was as fastidious over his sea-tackle-come-pike-conversion-rods and so on as the most avid fly fisherman with his delicate tackle, and he even went as far as carrying his frozen baits in an icebox to keep them solid, less likely to break up on the cast and capable of travelling farther. Were the rewards worth the effort? In one word, no. He caught no more fish than the rest of us, nor were his fish any bigger overall. In fact, the best pike taken from the pit he favoured most was taken by an angler deadbaiting along the reedbed bordering some shallows a mere 3m (10ft) from the side.

I gave up the long-distance chuck-it-and-chance-it tactics on stillwaters many years ago. Instead of concentrating on distance I now focus my attention on the topography of the water to be fished, especially that which lies below the surface, to an extent that if the water promises to be good then I will spend a day on examining and logging the place instead of using a rod and fishing. Nor am I alone in adopting this tactic, I gather, for the few expert pike anglers whom I am privileged to know well all, to some extent, use the same approach and make sure they know the underwater layout of prime waters that they fish, updating their knowledge at the commencement of each season.

Some interesting facts can emerge from this type of study. Gravel pits can look like a lunar landscape underwater when the dredgers have hauled ballast out and then dumped spoil back in its place, and occasionally the deeper holes and craters provide good fish. More often, however, I have found that a long channel of any reasonable width will be a better and more profitable proposition. I can call to mind one real hot spot where a gully some 7·6m (25ft) long and 0·9m (3ft) wide was situated just 13·7m (15yd) from a bank, and overlooked by all who fished there.

Channels leading to sluicegates, areas on ornamental lakes where wildfowl are regularly fed, large beds of well-established water lilies after the surface growth has died back to leave an underwater jungle of roots, drainage ditches that bring freshwater into that which is still, thus promoting weed growth and shoals of small fry – there are a dozen or more such places to watch for and always I find that they not only produce fish, but that they are rarely situated way out in the centre of the water, requiring marathon casting by the angler.

The skilful angler will know and appreciate those places where good pike may be found and he will also know the best method to be used for their capture; rarely, however, will repeated success be enjoyed where the fisherman is wedded to one single style. What succeeds on one day will fail the next. What is success for one water may well be failure for another.

Elsewhere I have proclaimed my love for float-fishing and nowhere can this be better practised than where the water lies still. But there is much also to be said for the paternoster, especially where the water is new to the angler and unexplored. Then some judicious casting and retrieving will quickly give some idea not only of the depth to the water but also the state of the bed, the solid 'thunk' of a weight against gravel contrasting with the sluggish drag of a weight being pulled across the mud.

Deep water, say over 4·5m (15ft) or so, usually responds well to a paternostered bait providing the rod tip is kept raised. There is only one successful method of doing this and Fig 9 shows it in practice. A length of piping sealed at one end is brazed to a metal rest and the rod is stepped handle-end first inside it. One of the plastic line clips holds

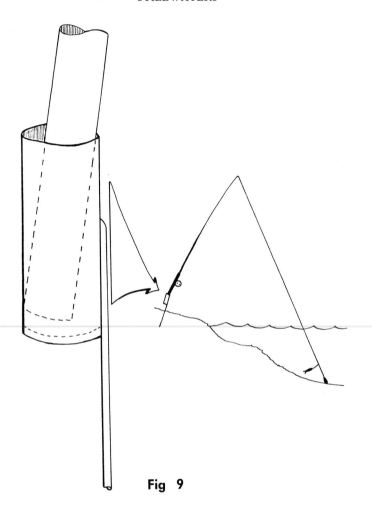

Fig 9

line between reel and first rod ring firm, allowing immediate release, providing, of course, that the bale arm or release button on the reel is kept open.

I often find myself at odds with fellow anglers on the question of fishing style on stillwaters. While the majority favour the sit-and-wait stance I am all for the seek-and-find style. The less I have to carry the better I like it and when you are on the move you rapidly dispense with excess baggage. You also quickly find a higher return in terms of runs and landed fish.

Difficult waters can be an enormous challenge. One I recently attempted was a moat where leaves which had fallen over several centuries had reduced the depth to an average of 45cm (18in) or so, which for some strange reason had driven even the most enthusiastic pikeman away, though the water was reputed to hold good pike. I fished the place on a day of gusting wind using one of the ET floats that drifted an air-inflated deadbait from one bank across to the other, where it searched against the stunted reed stems standing like shell-torn relics from a wartime bombardment. Before the dark and driving rain sent me to warmth and food I had banked eleven pike from 1·3–7·2kg (3–16lb) – and that sort of day has been repeated on innumerable occasions since then.

As readers will have gathered by now I am a man of few rigs either plain or fancy. I do use one, however, that takes me through those difficult days of early and high summer when weedgrowth is at its peak, not lilies and other floating vegetation but the sub-surface growth that reaches from the bed to about mid-water, especially where the water is deep. This is prime ground for summer pike fishing but only if you can suspend a bait just above or resting on the weed itself. The paternoster and ordinary float rigs tend to drag or pull the baits under cover, but the rig shown in Fig 10 prevents this aggravation.

A length of sub-breaking-strain line is secured to a lead or piece of scrap which will lie on the bottom with its other end secured to the float. Line from the reel is carried through the other ring of the bubble-float, to which in turn is attached the normal trace and deadbait rig. The link swivel at the trace end prevents the bait from jamming against the float. In use, the rig is allowed to run freely from the reel to allow the bait to drop below the surface. The depth at which the bait is to be fished can be controlled by a stop rigged from nylon overhand knots and a bead, or the bait can be allowed to free-fall and descend vertically into the weeds, the style I most use. In nine cases out of ten the bait will rest on the weed – and this is where it is most killing.

Once only have I been fortunate enough to actually see this rig score, and then through polarized glasses in fairly shallow water. The small dead roach descended to lie on a bed of pondweed that hung about a metre (3ft) under the surface. I watched for some time before a shape gently parted the weeds and stole the bait into oblivion. Away went the line, and a fish was on. But the interesting thing was not the size of the pike landed, which has been forgotten, but the fact that the *jaws only* appeared from the weeds to devour the bait. Not once did the fish

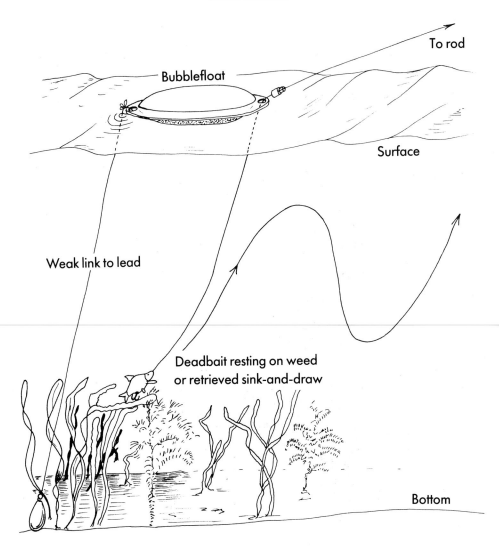

Fig 10 (Not to scale)

show itself and few, if any, anglers would have considered that a fish could possibly have been lying so well hidden.

It was dead, or, rather, still-waters that awoke my interest in groundbaiting for pike and most of my attempts at practising this fascinating subterfuge, one incidentally on which little serious research has been attempted, have been on large lakes and gravelpits where the freeloaded offering will stay in one position. My ideas on the subject originated with matchfishing when a well-baited swim would often be ravaged by pike, generally more than one, which would cut into small roach and dace that were attracted by the loose handfuls of groundbait spread in front of the peg.

Great cartwheels of fry in all shapes and sizes would erupt from the surface and then the swim would often die a death for an hour or more while the fish settled down or, worse, a hooked fish would be seized and held long enough for the angler to feel that he had a chance of landing and removing the inquisitor from the swim once and for all, only to see those flattened jaws open and release the victim before it could be landed, which definitely would not be fit for the weight-in. So, loose baiting to attract small fish became the prime groundbaiting method used during the summer and early autumn months and some good pike were taken with the aid of this simple ruse. But of course the method was of little use during real winter weather when fry and even larger fish cease to shoal and move around. It was then that the idea of using dead fish was tried and not surprisingly found wanting. Just lobbing out cut-up herring or halved sprats into the water was extremely 'chuck-it-and-chance-it', giving no guarantee that the offering would land anywhere near the hook bait. If you watch the movement of a loose piece of dead fish thrown into clear water you will quickly see how it can twist and turn, often landing some distance from where it entered the surface. More especially is this true where the water is deep and of course one may be fishing at such a distance from the bank that simply throwing loose offerings out towards the bait could be a waste of time because they would not get that far.

The natural follow-on was to consider baiting a relatively small area heavily then casting into it, and this is where the rubby-dubby trials commenced. The idea was that a large supply of fishmonger's offal could be used to spread the message of good food over a selected area, the offal held together in one of the brussels sprout net bags that greengrocers use when they purchase their sprouts in bulk.

We, for Adrian Lawson, my colleague of many gravelpit outings, was coerced into the action, tried the concept out on a Hertfordshire gravelpit where the working had left a long arm stretching out from the bank (Fig 11), rather like a harbour breakwater.

Using a large ball of string, one end was taken and attached to the netful of plaice bones, cods' heads and other delicacies. Then the string was paid out from the bank to the end of the 'breakwater' and back again before being attached to the other end of the net. This left an

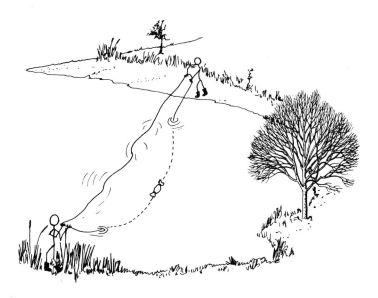

Fig 11

endless belt, so to speak, from bank to breakwater (some 40m (130ft)) and with one operator at either end it was an easy matter to haul the bag into the middle of the bay where, after some juggling backwards and forwards to spread the scent, the whole thing was allowed to come to rest. At the end of the day when fishing had ceased the bag would be retrieved and removed.

During the course of the day some vigorous working of the bag helped to keep the oily scent stirred while we fished deadbaits around the area – and the whole thing was reasonably successful. Pike fed but there were reservations on the ability of the method to produce fish at every outing. After a number of trials we began to realise that much depended upon the temperature of the water, which could have an adverse effect on the 'advertising' produced by the rubby-dubby bag. The warmer days produced a fair oil slick on the surface, which proved that there was circulation and also an improvement on the number of fish on the bankside. Very cold weather still produced a slick that

Late evening during a wet, cold winter's day. This fish took a tiny sprat and when landed, bumped the scales to 13·6kg (30lb) with ease. It was too late to get another, bigger set and the fish had to be returned. To my dying day I shall wonder how much it really weighed. The story is told in Chapter 6

showed the scent was permeating, but not to the degree produced by the warmer water. There was also some minus points to the method, which eventually led to the idea fading out and being dropped – at least by us. Not only were the extra fish that we were taking on the small side, with a large number in the 2·2–2·7kg (5–6lb) range, but actually carrying the dreadful and terrible offal to the waterside was not only a nuisance but positively lethal to clothing and the olfactory system. The whole idea came to a rapid end on the day that Adrian travelled up to the gravelpit by train. He had a large carrier bag full of the worst that his local fishmonger could offer and when he boarded the train Adrian set it fair and square on the luggage rack opposite him. Come the time to leave the train he lifted it down only to have the bottom fall out of the bag and spray its contents over a charming and well-groomed party of young girls on their way to school and who were sitting on the seat below the rack . . . .

Pike are not the only fish that show tendencies towards a carnivorous diet. A successful day of tench fishing, using blood from our local abbatoir mixed with ground breadcrumbs, set me thinking along the lines of spreading it, rather like a mist, across the bottom of the water as an attraction to pike. But the thought of carrying large amounts of breadcrumb and blood just did not spark off much enthusiasm: there always seems more than enough tackle to carry when piking without looking for further items.

There seemed to be a solution to the problem by using frozen blood and so, by way of experiment, two ice-cube dishes were filled with undiluted blood, a lead weight was dropped into each partition and the trays were left until frozen solid. Carrying was by means of a wide-mouthed vacuum flask and this kept the cubes solid until they were required for use. It was a partial success, and the blanket effect could to some degree be effected in deep water; but on the shallow stretches there was a tendency for the stuff to drift up to the surface, especially when the sun warmed the water. In fact, every experiment bar one that I have made with fluid groundbaits for piking has proved to be at the mercy of temperature, cold tending to keep the attractor in a small area, warmth quite quickly dispersing the offering over a wider area but unfortunately also drawing the mix to the surface.

An 8-pounder taken at a Thames weirpool during autumn. The slacker water at the tail of the pool itself is grand for sport at that time. Note the red-and-white plug – it represents nothing in the wild that a pike could ever see, but still attracts; whether from temper or curiosity we shall never know

The ice-cube method seemed to be successful, or at least we felt that more fish than usual were taken by using it but of course one can only prove that success is achieved in anything of this nature by knowing the total of fish that one would have caught without its assistance. And there were still some awkward angles to the method, such as freezing, for the family certainly did not take kindly to my using the freezer for such a gory mixture, and carrying the cubes meant added weight via the thermos flask and the need to use the supply early in the day.

A magazine article on eel fishing that extolled the virtues of using pilchard oil as a groundbait brought to mind a similar use for pike baiting. I gave the idea some thought and started by using a large swim-feeder packed with cottonwool soaked in the oil, and attached to the lead end of a paternoster rig. In theory the oil would wash out into the surrounding water, below where the bait would be suspended. In practice the old problem of cold water again prevented the thick oil from really washing out of the container. Of course, the process could be helped by jigging the rig up and down in the water but that rather transformed the style of fishing from that of live or deadbaiting into a form of sink-and-draw spinning.

My local chemist, equally at home dispensing for sick horses and farmyard animals as for human beings, came to the rescue. After I described the problem to him he recommended that I mix Polysorbate 80 with the thick oil in order to dilute its viscosity and then sink it. He made up a small quantity for me, but I nearly passed out when he gave me the bill. Then I recovered a little when it was explained that polysorbate was the stuff used by seaside councils to clear oil from the beaches and to sink crude mixture while it was still offshore, and that only a very small quantity would be required.

So I experimented and came up with a solution of one 5 ml teaspoon of polysorbate to 3 fl oz of pilchard oil, mixed and poured into an airtight bottle where it was well shaken before use. Carried in the bag there was no smell and it was reasonably safe. At the same time I designed a better unit for dispensing the stuff underwater, finding that there was a tendency for the cottonwool to fly out of the open ends of a swimfeeder during the cast. Using the plastic cannister supplied with a 35 mm film I punched a series of holes in its side and along the solid end, making a small hole through the lid and attaching this to the body by means of a loose plastic tie which also secured a clip-on swivel. Photograph 17 shows the finished product, it might be crude to look at, but it is cheap and effective.

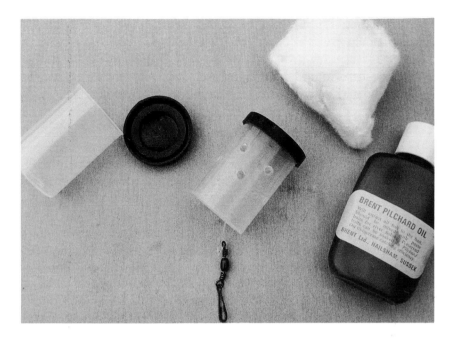

17 *This is the groundbait container that was manufactured from a plastic 35mm film cassette holder. The cotton wool filling is soaked with pilchard oil, punched holes allowing the water to enter. It is attached to the weight of a paternoster rig by a link swivel*

Fastened to the paternoster or leger weight, filled with cottonwool and primed with a teaspoonful or so of the 'polypilch' mixture, it allowed the fluid to slowly free itself and then to filter around the container, where its viscosity was such that it clung to the bottom. And the more casts made into a small radius the better and more efficient the attraction of the baiting became. Again, one can only really guess at the success of this experiment in groundbaiting. I felt that it was a help, especially on waters where overfishing made pike shy of anything approaching a deadbait – and sadly this is a condition rapidly extending to many popular waters. I have regularly taken fish using the method which does not, in the confines of my description, take up too much time or cause too much mess. But I feel that there are some slight constraints. The cold weather does tend to slow anything of a fatty or oily nature from spreading over a really wide area, no matter how well you work and attempt to spread the gospel, so to speak.

But the main risk I found came from the never-ending attacks during warm and some not-so-warm months made by eels, which seem almost to come from the adjoining counties, drawn there by the oil-filled water and which fastened onto a deadbait – which, of course, tends to suggest there are a few points in favour of using a livebait, except that with a livebait one should not need to groundbait; either way the angler just cannot win!

Running water is a different proposition. Here, the polypilch mixture and the self-designed groundbait cannister used with a paternoster can pay a handsome dividend, more especially when fishing deep holes and areas where one wants to draw a fish into the open, away from bad snags. But beware of fastening too many gadgets to the end of the line when fishing really fast water. Inefficiency outrules possible attraction and extra clutter combines so often to cause time-wasting tangles.

Any frustration that I may have experienced while experimenting with groundbaiting for pike was nothing when compared with my utter frustration at trying to understand hotspots. And judging from my many bankside conversations I am not alone in this bewilderment.

What exactly is a hotspot? Is it a place where a number of pike pack-hunt, clustering together to drive against fish that they require for food, in the manner in which German submarines pack-hunted during World War II? Or is it a place where a constant food supply is present, allowing pike to collect and feed without the effort of chase and capture? In Chapter 5 I described a hotspot area on the Thames which, I felt, was produced by ample cover that gave protection to pike from predators, and showed the food supply to advantage. But, having acknowledged that particular place I can think of others where the reverse could apply and there was little cover and sometimes positive danger to pike which hid in the hotspot, and just would not keep away.

I think the first thing we must acknowledge is that a hotspot is a place where pike can habitually be found and that means more than one fish and from more than one position in the water. Normally, hotspots are associated with stillwaters and the area will usually be found to be a fairly small one. And by and large those 'hot' areas remain constant – I only know of two places where pike have, for reasons that I have not been able to explain, disappeared completely.

18 *The edge of this small reedbed is a real hotspot. Many pike, similar to the one of over 13.6kg (30lb) shown in the colour photograph on page 103, have been taken from swims where the water is only a metre (3ft) or so deep*

Photographs 18–22 show some of the hotspots that I have fished and it may be interesting to examine and describe some of them – certainly their characteristics are anything but constant.

A typical bankside to a lake is shown in Photograph 18. The water is situated in the depths of Wales and consistently produces pike in the 11·3–13·6kg (25–30lb) range. The whole lake is unreal to the unprepared angler in that it has just about the highest food count in terms of insect life and water vegetation that I have ever encountered. There are seven independent springs feeding into various sections, the pH value is spot on – neutral – and all the species of fish that it holds are not only in excellent condition but run into record-breaking weights. The water that can be seen in front of the angler is barely a metre (3ft) deep, and is bordered by a reedbed that remains in a wrecked state throughout the winter whatever the weather. Beyond that there is not one unusual area of outstanding underwater topography other than the bed itself, which is of gravel, evenly spread with a little leafmould in places. Yet this is a hotspot that will produce three, sometimes four fish at an outing and always to the smallest of deadbaits, usually sprats, the fish often coming in such quick succession that the water has scarcely ceased to boil from the capture of the first fish before the next is onto the hooks. Why?

I remained puzzled for some time until one day my tackle became caught in the reeds while I was retrieving a plug. It was at the end of the day and rather than lose tackle I waded out to release things – and two arrow shapes shot out into the open water, towards the centre of the lake. Immediately all became clear: that hotspot was formed by pike which lay among the reeds for shelter. I also had an explanation of why a bait fished farther than the edge of the reeds, or outside of a band running parallel with them, some 2·4m (8ft) or so wide and about 9m (30ft) long at the most, failed to score. The answer was that the pike could not see it!

Strangely, springs were the key to the pike in the colour photograph (page 103). This fish came from a lake way up in the Cambrian mountains that was just about the most desolate place I have ever fished in my life – and that includes the outback in Australia. The place was well above sea level and though of great size when compared with lowland lakes it provided nothing in the way of enormous cover from weed or even a large insect count, something which usually indicates abundant shoals of small fry and ultimately pike food.

There was one small corner that soon registered as a pike hotspot, yet I could see no reason for this. Then quite by chance I noticed a small spring feeding into the bay, something quite common in the Principality. On one session, fishing on the coldest winter day I can remember, I was surprised to find that the water in that spot was relatively warm and I made a check with a thermometer over several outings in the weeks that followed. This proved that the water in the bay there could be as much as 2°C higher than the rest of the lake. It was not much, but it was enough to draw fish into the area and hold them there either through an interest in feeding on fry or from sheer 'appreciation' of that little extra warmth.

The pike in the photograph, incidentally, has caused me more sleepless nights since its capture than I care to think about. The fish took a very small deadbait just as dusk was fallling and gave me a hefty tussle that lasted until the light had nearly gone. Once onto the bank I weighed it carefully with the aid of a colleague. But the Salter spring balance bounced down to the 13·6kg (30lb) limit with a bang that left me in no doubt that the fish weighed considerably more. But what to do? The farmhouse was 9·6km (6 miles) away, darkness had fallen, so all that could be done ultimately was to slide the fish back again and hope to join forces with it on a future outing. And that, of course, has never happened, though there is not a day that passes during the pike season during which I do not wonder just how much more that fish really did weigh above 13·6kg (30lb).

The scene in Photograph 19 is interesting. It is of a small private stillwater that nowhere runs deep, but which contains pike up to 6·8kg (15lb) which have splendid markings and fight like dervishes. The photograph was taken at a time when the water had been lowered for repairs to a flood sluicegate; the middle distance shows a narrow bank of gravel and mud that stretches from one bank to the other. It is a hotspot, not only on either side of the raised spit but actually on top of the gravel and mud bank even though there is often no more than 0·6m (2ft) of water covering it.

I fished and watched this area for several seasons before a possible explanation of its popularity came to light. Talking to one of the local council workers I discovered that the raised bank covered a sewage

Overleaf **19** *Hotspots can be totally puzzling. Pike in this partly-drained moat can be caught over the raised shoulder running out from the bank in mid-picture. It is shallow, exposed, without shelter, but never without a pike in residence. The secret lay in what was below the ridge – warm water running through a pipe below it*

system which ran from a village (off to the right of the photograph) to a mains sewer away beyond and to the lefthand bank. Of course, this system carried warm water as well as cold and the heat, small though it might have been, was felt by the coarse fish which lodge around the area and which in turn are fed upon by the pike. Photograph 20 shows Thorpe Park, near Virginia Water, Surrey, the Thorpe Belle being a restaurant built in the style of a Mississippi riverboat supported on piles out over the water. I went to photograph activities there when the water was open to pike fishermen for two days and soon discovered that the place where fish were consistently being taken was just in front, or to one side of the imitation boat that can be seen in the background. Fish after fish was caught, and those of us nearby soon realised that the underside of the boat-cum-café was packed full of pike in the small jack to 7·2kg (16lb) bracket.

Why, again? A possible clue was that the day was one of cloudless skies with a superbright winter sun that drove deep into the frost-cleared water. Pike do not like it – it was my early experience at Teddington again (see Chapter 7) – and they were taking advantage of the cover that was being offered by the boat. And when food was dropped nearby in the form of deadbaits the results were a foregone conclusion. But of course, in the strictest sense of the word one could not designate the area as a true hotspot because fish very probably moved out into other areas when dull skies became prevalent once more.

Let us now discuss a mobile hotspot or, rather, hotspots in the plural. Photograph 21 shows a killick – a drainage ditch – on the Pevensey Marshes during high summer. As with all still or nearly still waters the dreaded duckweed spreads its blanket during the summer months until many of the waters are covered, or nearly so. To ignore the area is to leave a profitable source of summer piking, but to fish through the stuff is like fishing through ink. One cannot see, or even imagine what is happening beneath the surface.

20 *Another hotspot. It was a bright winter's day at Thorpe Aquadrome when this pike, one of a dozen or so, was caught from beneath the mock riverboat. The reason was that this is one of the few areas of shade and sheltered water on the gravelpit*

21 *The edge of a dreaded duckweed bed. The fringes where this weed leads into clear water often contain a pike, the fish using the green surface blanket as protection*

Quite by chance I fished the edge of one of the duckweed clouds without success of any kind until I retrieved the bait, which was a small roach fished deadbait-style and free-lined: a killing summer method on marshland waters. As the bait came to the surface just beside the green and wavy edge of the duckweed it was seized by a jack of 3·1kg (7lb), a fish that put up an enormous fight as so many of the late summer pike do. I recast and fished again without success, only to score once more as the bait was being brought slowly to the surface. This time it was a pike of 4kg (9lb) and I immediately realised that there was every chance that more fish would follow, if not from that area then from a similar one. And so it proved, for of course the wide, barren landscape was being given the sun treatment and pike were lying just under the duckweed, shaded but able to see into the surrounding area, keen on feeding but yet not quite making an acknowledged year-round hotspot.

It is an excellent summer standby and one that repays serious fishing with a well-inflated deadbait that floats, or lies nearly on top of the surface. Those anglers, incidentally, who have never had a floating bait taken by a pike have a pleasure to come. The smash and turn of even a small pike can create an enormous disturbance and cause the heart to miss several beats.

The heavy vegetation shown in Photograph 22 provides an interesting comparison with the normal definition of a hotspot. The water shown is a tiny Sussex stream that, at the time it was taken, was at its normal summer flow. The water is full of pike, but they become very 'iffey' under these conditions and one cannot be sure of a fish at any outing unless the small area shown in the photograph is fished, using either live or deadbait, which must be worked and held under the overhanging weeds growing from the opposite bank. Then, without fail, a pike will leap out as it were and practically swallow fish and angler in one gulp despite the fact that the water is shallow. Not necessarily a big fish every time but *always* a pike and for a reason that I cannot fathom. There are a dozen similar tiny bays on the water, same depth, amount of cover – everything uniform on the fishery at that time of year, but there is just that one place to repeatedly score. It is not a hotspot, perhaps, but a lifesaver for a day out, with a reason for popularity with the pike that I am still trying to solve.

To sum up the question of hotspots. Basically, I believe that they are where pike collect, perhaps a deep area in surrounding shallows, a place of deeper colour against which their own colour mutations will blend and so give them safety, or an area where the water is less likely to be affected by cold or which may be well-sheltered from the direct sun. Hotspots can also be places where food is plentiful and where it need not be relentlessly pursued, but that, in my experience, appears to be rather low on the list of a pike's natural and instinctive priorities.

If there is one fault with hotspots it lies with their becoming known to anglers in general. From the moment of discovery they will be relentlessly fished even to the extent of round-the-clock coverage. Despite that fact that it will be fished out, it will continue to attract anglers merely because so many fishermen confuse the word 'hotspot' with 'suicidal surrender'. These places need as much careful and considerate handling and angling tactics as any other area, something never to be allowed to slip the mind. Hotspots I have found in recent years have been by deduction and not chance, and I take good care to keep them to myself for reasons that will be discussed more fully in the final chapter to this book.

Of the many pleasures that can be found in piking, that of spinning or plug fishing in stillwaters, must be the greatest. Again, it is the mobility of the style that appeals to me, a freedom to wander and work with fresh water to be examined at every step, whole banksides to be analysed and worked over with the rod. Given a cold winter's day, a large expanse of water and good company no sportsman could ask for more.

My approach to large stillwaters is to use the multiplying reel with the rod that was designed to work with it but which is so little used now that it has fallen practically into disuse. It is the rod that is fitted with a cranked handle. This small detail of construction produces an efficiency of casting and fish playing that has only to be experienced before one completely surrenders to the mode. Many moons ago I had a 2·4m (8ft) glassfibre rod fitted with a double-handed handle and I have never regretted the money I parted with at the time, nor would I ever part with that rod.

Fished correctly, rod rings and reel uppermost, this outfit when matched with balancing line and lure can equal the most accurate rifle and place a bait to the inch without hitch or tangle. When the water is

Overleaf **22** *This small, vegetation-crowded stream would be overlooked by the majority of anglers. But it is an excellent summer fishery where lightweight tackle and quiet tactics produce good fish. A pike of 3.6kg (8lb) has been caught from the gap in front of the angler*

small, making large lures not only unnecessary but even counter-productive, then the 2·4m (8ft) lightweight straight-handled spinning rod with Fuji rings and screw winch fittings, matched with a closed face reel, will be found equally delightful and accurate using tiny lures. But there is one set of geographical features in stillwaters which causes me to reach for a bigger, more sophisticated outfit. On occasions, a water will be found where the depth is extreme, and by that I mean well over 6m (20ft), sometimes down to 10·6m (35ft). Now, try as one might, it is all but impossible to persuade a lure to run that deep, no matter how long the area of retrieve will be. Reel in like a dervish and even the biggest lip fitted to a deep-diving plug, or the heaviest spinner you can muster, will neither run down nor run parallel to the bottom.

The answer? It is back to the paternoster rig again, much as described in Chapter 5, but instead of allowing the current to stream the lure and make it work, the angler must retrieve and pull the rig through the water. Awkward? Yes, at first sight. But somehow the lead dragging across the bottom seems partially to act as an attractor rather than a deterrent. The stream of particles and mud that clouds upwards can, it seems, bring out the inquisitiveness in a pike which will lead to the lure being taken firmly as it follows the 'smoke screen', always provided that the angler varies the depth at which he fishes the lure by altering the distance between lead and trace and does not just keep the lure constantly at the same depth. The best lures? Those with which you are familiar and that you use day after day with success and, above all, those that you have confidence in. My experience has shown big lures to score on dark days and vice versa, but at the same time much will depend not on the overall size of the water you are fishing but on the depth. Do not be frightened to experiment, either. A dozen mackerel lasks, long, narrow triangular strips cut from the side of the fish and packed into a small, airtight box, can work wonders when one is hung from the end treble of a spinner or plug. And do not be in a hurry to stop and pack your rods away when fishing on stillwaters where it is allowed after dark. Many a good fish has been caught at last light and, even more often, after complete darkness has fallen and when most pikemen have gone home.

I have found this more especially on waters that are really fished hard, with anglers tramping up and down and generally doing their best to show themselves to the fish. It seems that pike are aware when anglers have left and then come out to feed in comparative safety. But be prepared for the darkness. It is no use fumbling about trying to unhook a fish when you cannot see it, nor is it fair on the fish. Knife-and-fork work done blindly results in fish that are found floating belly up on the following morning and that does nothing for the image of pike anglers, or for the unfortunate pike. But the best and the worst days fishing are all, to some extent, governed by the weather, which is something completely beyond our control. That weather exerts an influence on fishing by encouraging pike to feed; move around; stop feeding; lie dormant, goes without saying. What is in doubt is what does which and when. I have read many learned articles and chapters in books and magazines on this subject and studied carefully the words of the masters who felt capable of stating without equivocation what this or that state of the barometer, degree of temperature, amount of light will produce. And I do not believe a word of what I read. And I state that for two very excellent reasons. One is that I can remember occasions when I have caught fish on just about every type of bad weather that those experts described, when fish just were not supposed to be interested in feeding. And secondly, even if I knew that conditions were such that fish would probably not feed during the day I would still go pike fishing, and so would just about every other red-blooded pikeman worthy of his name. It would be an odds-on chance of taking a fish, but that makes one more determined to succeed, keen to study the water and tactics, and concentrate that degree or so harder to produce results.

I am very well aware of the type of weather that bring a confidence to my pike fishing (and that in itself is something to promote success) and I also know weather that I dislike. But before I start to discuss performances and preferences allow me to agree with the general description of good pike fishing weather, which is that sport will generally be good at times of high barometric pressure. But having said that it would be as well to say that such pressure can vary over a very short distance. In the days when I thought I was smart and of sufficient genius to shake the pike fishing world with great scientific discoveries I carried a barometer and logged a reading on each outing. It was only when I took two readings on the same day, at either end of the Pevensey Marshes that I found a difference of nearly an inch in pressure, and began to appreciate that weather could not be neatly pigeon-holed and that success and failure would, as it always has done, rest in the hands of the Gods.

Let my opening chapter to this book describing my outing on the Pevensey Levels start the ball rolling on weather and fishing. A stretch of really open weather had suddenly ended while I was out in it, with the dawn sun suddenly being obliterated by low cloud, and a feeling that a violent change of weather was on the way: something foretold by the sudden and complete silence that descended across the marsh. It indicated a falling barometer and combined with a fall in temperature was not the sort of weather one would not lay money on for taking a fish. But I scored and so have I on other occasions when this sudden change has occurred. It would almost seem that fish are aware of the hardships to come and feed accordingly, but that is too neat an explanation!

I would have been happier still on that day with an increase in the wind, for wind is one of the best portents to sport that I know of in pike fishing. It is damned annoying when casting and miserable when it is cold and piercing, but the ripple to the surface, the move of water, not only hides the angler but also must embody an increase in oxygen which is important and rewarding. Rain is another weather saviour to the pikeman and I have known occasions when a sudden heavy squall has woken every pike imaginable and set them on the feed, a factor due again in no small way to an increase in oxygen to the water, I am sure. Another good pike weather portent for me is soft light. I suppose that as a photographer I am more than usually aware of light values and time and again I have noticed that when there is that soft, filling light that illuminates but does not produce harsh shadow, then the day will usually turn out well.

But the best of all, weather that sends blood coursing round the body and whets the anticipation, is to arrive at the waterside and find a rising mist or light fog. Most anglers will know what I mean, and will, like myself, have had excellent sport when the float rides through wraiths of mist or the spinner falls and works beyond the sight of the angler. And when the mist is rising because the water is warm and then, later, the air temperature rises to meet that of the water itself some of the best sport can be expected.

What do I dislike? The gin-clear water after prolonged and heavy frost when you can see the bait lying like the lost city of Atlantis on the bottom really deep below the surface. Though having said that I will retract a little and admit that I have had some good times spinning in such clarity – but not while using the stationary dead or livebait.

Incidentally, fish taken at that time are unusual in their fighting mode. Whereas the pike hooked in temperatures above freezing will move around and fight over a distance, those hooked in intense cold seem to fight in a circle without moving more than a few feet from where they are first hooked. Why, I do not know, but one must wonder whether it is not unconnected with some kind of torpor brought on by the fall in temperature.

Hard sunlight is another of my dislikes and when I switch on the lightmeter and the needle shoots into high figures my heart sinks, for I know I could be on a hiding to nothing. Finally, there is the time following prolonged rain when the water is stained dark, a murky colour and full of sediment. One can score with a plug or spinner but often it is a fish-beater. But watch for that water to clear – then some excellent sport can await, with the pike feeding voraciously.

7
Tidal Waters

It was one of Adolf Hitler's bombers during World War II that led to my becoming interested in pike fishing in tidal waters. Before the event I, like most other anglers, would never have considered that pike could exist in what the freshwater fisherman prefers to call 'adulterated' water. The bomber which caused my forward thinking dropped its high-explosive cargo over the Thames at Teddington on one dark night and one of the bombs struck the weir that marks the limit of the tideway and the beginning of freshwater. The damage to the weir was considerable and some temporary repairs had been carried out. The old wooden structure had been propped and shored with no attempt to fill the crater left when the bomb exploded, and on the tidal side a deep, wide half-circular hole still gaped in the concrete weir apron. It produced a deep swim that made a natural haunt for small dace and roach at low water, filling and overflowing as the tide rose to bring better fish in, including bream and an occasional carp. The swim became a popular one and anglers would line the sides, fishing until the rising water flooded everyone off and back to the banks below the weir. I counted twenty anglers there on one occasion, elbow to elbow without any hint of discord and every angler had fish to show for his efforts.

Towards the end of the war I came home on leave from the Royal Navy and went to the Thames at Teddington to regain some fishing time that had been lost. I tackled up by the crater on a cold, dark and windy Christmas Eve, in company with another angler who had decided, like myself, to brave the elements and enjoy nature's peace as opposed to the pace of Christmas. Upstream, several weir gates were drawn and millions of gallons of water made their way down towards the sea. As the tide rose the sport increased as roach and dace side-slipped or stabbed at our maggot-baited hooks until the gradually

124

making tide seeped up to our feet, reminding us that a move would soon have to be made. I stopped fishing momentarily to gather my tackle together, then my attention was taken as the other fisherman's cork-on-quill float dipped from the pull of another sizeable roach. As the fish struggled a slim, dark-green body appeared and sliced at the fish, turning away with the roach and the hook in its mouth. The rod bent, off went the check of the Nottingham reel and the fight commenced.

After 15 minutes or so things were desperate as the rising tide climbed to the tops of our wellingtons, but there is only so much pressure that can be applied to 1·3kg (3lb) breaking strain silk line and fine silkworm gut. We had just reached the cut-and-run decision when a pike of about 2.7kg (6lb) turned over on to its side, beaten and ready to be landed. With a good deal of trepidation I took the small, shallow landing net that was the vogue then, when nobody dared admit to fishing for anything bigger than a 0·9kg (2lb) roach, and tried frantically to fit the pike into the small-framed net: it gave a flick of its tail and was off. So we grabbed our now-floating tackle bags, clambered to the bank, emptied the water from our wellingtons and reflected as countless other anglers have done over the years that there 'ain't no angling justice!'

The incident was interesting, but it was forgotten until the following summer when I fished from one of Harry Bishop's punts moored out in the weirpool at Teddington, Harry was a professional Thames fisherman who had spent a lifetime on the water, an acknowledged expert on fish, fishing and most other things connected with the Thames. The day was idyllic, blue sky, warm sun and good fishing. I was moored comfortably across the stream and had only to let the float go at my feet and it would long-trot away downstream without effort on my part. I had plenty of maggots and was feeding them as groundbait through an aluminium tube that had been lowered over the upstream side of the punt and fixed so that its end was just above the bottom. A handful fed into the top end every five minutes provided a trickle of goodies that drifted downstream at exactly the right depth.

Halfway through the morning I noticed a burst of silvery fry as the small fish flung themselves out of the water against a wall that now forms the bank to Thames Television studios away on the left. When the same thing happened again I thought that a good-sized Thames trout was responsible for the panic and cast out a bleak mounted on a single hook through the lip to investigate. It was supported on a fat celluloid float that helped work it along and through the shadows made by the brickwork. In the course of an hour I had had three takes and lost as many livebaits without connecting with the fish that was responsible for those sudden, fast, down-sweeps of my large float. At lunchtime, Harry rowed out and took me off for a liquid lunch at the Tide End Cottage and over a pint I told him of my bad luck. He put me right by explaining that the 'trout' had probably been a pike, of which there were plenty along the tideway down as far as Richmond. Harry had not seen them heavier than 5·4kg (12lb) and they were invariably caught from sheltered water where a fish could hide from bright sunshine, something Harry insisted that no pike on the tideway could exist without.

With hindsight, Harry's theory examined against the knowledge of the upward binocular vision that pike possess must be correct. Strong sunlight and shallow water could ruin vision and make a fish vulnerable to unseen danger. So began my interest in fishing for pike from tidal waters, different in many respects from sport in strictly freshwater areas yet equally fascinating but at times more aggravating. The chances of angling success when fishing this kind of water are governed by salinity. And there is a limit to the amount of saltwater that can be mixed with fresh before distress is caused to the pike there.

However, there are big pike – some over 15kg (33lb) – in the Baltic and the shallow bays and inlets hold huge numbers of smaller ones, showing that pike can tolerate a considerable salinity level in some areas. Very recently the Swedes made changes in their fishing laws so that anglers can now fish for these pike, thus opening enormous areas of virgin water.

I discussed the salinity problem with Dr Buckley, Fisheries Officer of the Southern Water Authority, and she gave a figure of about 5 per cent saltwater as the tolerance factor, above that there could be devastation and probable death to pike. The percentage seems small when compared with the pike in the Baltic, but it must be remembered that where de-oxygenation or pollution occur it is the pike that succumb first.

Now where does this figure of 5 per cent become 6 per cent along the river? Where is it that one can fish with a chance of sport, but below which the angler will be wasting his time? The question cannot be answered in simple terms because there are a number of factors to be taken into consideration. The varying tides, neaps and springs, will create their own limits, and the weather must also affect the demarcation line. Heavy rains which produce floods will send freshwater downstream and may encourage pike to travel beyond their usual stations. In severe floods, fish are literally forced downstream by the force of the current. Many are taken this way and some ultimately die; the first double-figure pike I ever saw was lying dead on a recently exposed bank of the Cockshut, a small tributary of the Sussex Ouse which had flash-flooded during a summer storm.

At the other extreme is summer low water and long periods of drought – 1984 was a recent example – where a reduced flow of freshwater drew fish back upstream of the tideway, packing them below weirs or lock gates that mark the cut-off between fresh and saline water – the magic 5 per cent mixture. So there is no hard and fast rule about the regular movements of pike along the tideway, it is anybody's guess. So far as I know, there is no accurate test that will save time being spent in fishing blank water. Tasting the water is no indication, because I have tried it a number of times. A problem equally disconcerting can be that of deciding where the pike lie, assuming that one has set up where the water will support them. In normal freshwater fishing the experienced angler will walk the banks and use his sixth sense that has developed over the years to assess where the fish will be. I concentrate on the salient features such as deep, slow bends, eroded banks, weedbeds and current fluctuations, all of which will subconsciously tell me 'There's the place!' But all those landmarks and water indications are largely absent on the tideway.

Let us take the matter of Teddington again. Here there is an ultra-wide section of river boasting weir and locks with a considerable current pushing downstream during the periods of low water, the tide pushing relentlessly back upstream again twice during a 24-hour period. This twice-daily movement has produced over time a gravel bed totally devoid of any significant weed growth and completely featureless apart from a central channel across the weirpool and down the main course of the Thames. There are now none of the variations which should provide holding places for pike, even the bomb crater has been filled in. This means that the pike will search for what little cover there is, such as the slack water produced by man-made features, principally round the edges of the weir, the supports of the bridges and lock walls and the lock cuttings themselves. These, in fact, are exactly the places where Harry Bishop suggested would provide 'shade' and protection for fish in a barren riverbed.

23 *The white, delicate underside of a pike's head and jaws. One wonders why the fish ever leaves the safety of the bottom to allow this brilliant white to expose the pike to other predators that may be lying below them. Of course, if there is brilliant sunlight above, much of the pike's outline will be lost against the glare of the hard light*

It is fortunate that this lack of cover appears to have little effect on pike numbers, for I have seen and caught many fish from the tideway areas of cover. Many have not been easy to tempt into taking a bait and any casual 'I'll stick out a livebait' approach rarely succeeds. My success in catching my early pike is due to Harry Bishop's excellent advice for I had long wanted to solve the problem of catching those pike along the weir wall which had eluded me. The first thing was that I needed to use a boat and someone to row it if I was going to get the best from the situation. At that time the charge for a punt was 10s 6d (52½p) a day without a boatman, but his presence doubled the cost to a guinea (£1.05p). This may appear cheap when compared with today's prices, but at the time it represented the better part of a week's wages. Harry sensed my predicament and offered me half a day's fishing with his help for 7s 6d (37½p) on the condition that any fish I caught were returned immediately. Keen as he was to see good angling sport, Harry was one of the strongest advocates of conservation on the

Thames, an unusual characteristic in the days of large gaffs and crude 'let 'im get it well down' methods, nothing more than semi-gorge tactics.

A late September afternoon saw us out in a light wooden skiff, Harry rowing up to the head of the weir, where he manoeuvred the boat across the current and in position a cast or two away from the wall. Late summer swallows dipped and swooped for flies as the anchor was lowered without a bump to the bottom. Using the traditional Jardine livebait tackle and float it was easy for me to longtrot a dace, the incoming tide taking it gracefully up against the brickwork. During the highwater period four pike came to the net, the best a little over 3·8kg (8½lb), Harry lifting the anchor and easing the boat quietly and soundlessly into a new position as each fish came inboard. Then the sport stopped as the tide dropped and the fish showed no interest in spite of regular renewals of bait to make sure they were working to the best advantage. Harry would not offer unsolicited fishing advice as he sat without comment until at last I asked for help. He searched through his pockets and brought out an ordinary bottle cork and said that as the tide dropped and the water became shallow a normal float with its usual weights would clearly be seen on the surface by fish. The bottle cork (something from the trout fisherman's tackle box) was slit up one side and pushed onto the line. With no weight the rig would not be so evident, the bait would swim beneath it and would be more likely to attract fish. That advice was sound but we had just one more pike, which weighed 2·7kg (6lb), that session.

Bank fishing could be found in the lock area with its dredged channel and among the projecting piles either side that led to the gated entrance. Here, one could – and still can – paternoster with a livebait during the winter months when pressure from boat traffic eases. This must be a pure paternoster with the rod tip near-vertical, not at an angle which produces a slanting drape on the line that indicates a somewhere-off-the-bottom style. One curious fact about using the paternoster in a tideway is that when the livebait fails to attract and defeat looms a change to a deadbait rigged head down and worked back sink-and-draw will often find a pike regardless of the state of the tide. The reason is probably because one works a deadbait in big up and down sweeps that provoke rather than attract, an action easily made in water that is weed-free and without many snags. My best pike from the Thames tideway came this way, one of 5kg (11lb) caught

129

near the lock gates at the entrance to what was Ham Gravel Pits, now the Young Mariners' Lock.

The comments I have made on legering should not be taken to indicate that I am not in favour of the style. Far from it, a specialized rig that I often use came into being as a direct result of some very off water conditions on the tideway. On occasion the half-tide lock at Richmond, below Teddington, is left open to allow repairs to be carried out along the lower reaches of the river and when this happens the term 'low water' takes on a totally new meaning. The water recedes and an area of the Thames at Teddington considered best for pike fishing is exposed and seen as an enormous sweep of empty gravel, the flow from the weir keeping within a rather wide central channel. This happened once in the early 1970s, when I arrived on a winter's day of faint sun and found near-impossible fishing conditions. It was a waste of time to think of pike fishing, so I legered – the only style possible – for roach and dace, my bait near a cluster of small boats moored in mid-stream and in the shadows of the main footbridge across the river. I intended to fish that way until the rising tide would provide enough water to make easier fishing. But twice a small fish I was bringing to the net was seized by a pike obviously sheltering under the moored boats and after lunging at my fish the pike would retreat to comparative safety.

My instinctive reaction to such fishy boldness was to float-fish a livebait out, but then decided that this was not the correct method. The casting distance would require fair weight and as the water was only about 0·9m (3ft) in the channel such a clumsy approach would receive the treatment it deserved and be ignored. A traditional leger or paternoster rig would be equally useless because a stationary bait close to the boats would not have the same effect as a bait that worked its way beneath them and into the pike's vision. I searched my tackle box and selected a round bullet with a wide hole drilled through the centre and to help the easy run of line through it I scraped more lead away from the hole, making it a bell-shape. With the bullet as an anchor I half-hitched a matchstick as a line-stop and completed the rig with a snap-tackle mounted with a freshly killed small bream cadged from a nearby angler.

Casting upstream of the boats I held the rod high and waited until I could feel the current pulling at the deadbait before paying line out to allow the bait to drift downstream, turning and swinging in the water in as natural way as possible. The weight helped me to maintain line control and prevented the rig being washed back into the sides of the channel. Soon I felt the pull from a taking fish and a small pike was out onto the bank and back in the water within a minute. It was not a big fish, size was not important; but what was of interest was the style that had accounted for its capture. I thought of that improvised rig for days afterwards, trying to see if I could improve it. It had to be able to allow a deadbait to work naturally and freely downstream on the current for a considerable distance without swinging back into the bank. The problem was to ensure that it drifted cleanly with no jerks or snatches, something that the bullet rig had suffered from at least once. It had to be guaranteed to work cleanly every time if the rig was to be a success, a soft riverbed, for instance, would quickly envelop the weight and halt the downstream progress of the bait.

Eventually the simple rig shown in Fig 12 was made. A plastic curtain ring 1cm (½in) in diameter was fastened by a short length of heavy 9kg (20lb) monofilament to an Arlesey bomb, a combination that would keep the ring well above the riverbed and comparatively tangle-free. Line from the reel passed through the ring and was stopped by a matchstick (which also floated and helped keep the line off the bottom) and below that was a small but strong link swivel to give easy attachment of the hook rig. Experiments with a bubblefloat or a cork fastened above the swivel to help the passage of the bait proved unnecessary, the bait moving with complete freedom as more

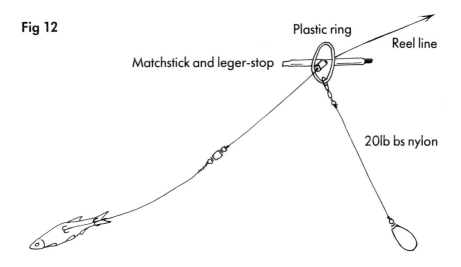

Fig 12

Plastic ring

Reel line

Matchstick and leger-stop

20lb bs nylon

and more line was paid out. A further trial using braided nylon with its floating property proved useless, the line would bow on the rod side of the plastic ring and travel ahead of the bait, which remained held by the matchstick stop.

This has become one of my standard rigs not only on tideways but in many other situations where a bait needs to be worked with help from the current. I often use it, too, in stillwaters where the bottom may be covered in weed, mud or – especially in early autumn – fallen leaves, which smother a normal leger rig.

So far as tideways are concerned, not every water has the same conditions as the Thames; there are plenty of tidal fisheries in this country where the pressure-flow of freshwater downstream is sufficiently strong to hold incoming saltwater at bay for as much as 1·6km (1 mile) or more, so that when the tide does rise little or no saltwater is carried upstream. The Hampshire Avon immediately springs to mind with its lush weed growth in an area normally considered tidal, but providing food and shelter for all species. Proof that freshwater is held at bay by saltwater can be found by examining the Hampshire Avon below Johnsons, above the famous Bridge Pool. Here weed comes to an end as if it has been cut by a knife, killed by the saltwater of near full-strength salinity that pushes to this point.

The only occasion in my life when I have knowingly poached was on the Royalty, that famous fishery on the Hampshire Avon, during the days when maggots used in enormous quantities were the vogue and scored as a bait. At the time I was, unsuccessfully, seeking barbel and fishing a swim below the Bypass Bridge. At about mid-afternoon it started to rain, driving the less stoic fishermen from the packed banks and giving the angling stalwarts plenty of room, so I walked down to Johnson's Pool looking for a fresh swim and passed a Birmingham lad packing up his gear. He pointed out a hole under tree roots on the opposite bank. He had baited the area all day and had seen the shape of a large fish that had moved out from the bank and snatched at some groundbait before sliding back under the tree roots. It was, he said, the biggest barbel on the Avon.

So I took over his swim, tackled up and soon had some small fish in the net. Then the rain cleared and the tide started to fill, bringing with it several mullet that ghosted through with the current. As I watched them a shape drifted away from the far bank, just as the angler had predicted. I saw the fish turn below the surface before sinking out of sight and there was no mistaking its outline in the gin-clear water: it was not a barbel, but a pike and a big one too. Now, on the Royalty there is no difference in price between ordinary coarse fishing and a ticket that includes pike. But fishing for pike is not allowed before November 1, and then by float-fishing only, all pike to be removed from the water. But a pikeman through and through, the challenge facing me was one that I could not resist: that fish had to be mine and there was only one thing to do. Moving back from the water I checked to see if the bailiff was about but saw no sign of him. There was spinning gear among my tackle, so I quickly removed the treble from a large spoon and mounted it on a somewhat worn spinning trace.

It occurred to me to try spinning for the pike, but I decided against it because it would not be possible to get a lure into the corner where the fish was, and added to that to be caught spinning on a game fishing river during the season without the correct licence would be at least a hanging offence. Instead, I fixed a rough paternoster rig, then killed a small roach and part-disembowelled it, leaving the guts hanging before mounting it by threading the trace through a gill slit and out through the mouth, securing the hook by one point in the dorsal fin area. This is a tried and tested but messy method and deadly when one wants to attract a pike from a difficult corner where it is not possible to work a natural or artificial lure. The bait must be suspended well above the bottom otherwise every eel in the vicinity will grab the hook; for the same reason a leger rig cannot be used.

I cast the deadbait out close to the dark tree roots opposite and kept my rod tip well up as I waited. I did not wait for long, then the pike moved out and took the bait. At this point I admit that I would not choose to fish for pike on the Avon with a Wallis-type split-cane rod designed for barbel and using 2·7kg (6lb) line. But my luck held and the incoming tide was stemming much of the flow that would have assisted a large, well-hooked pike. The strike was made and hoping that the tackle would hold I bullied the fish for a quarter of an hour and kept it in open water, eventually drawing it to the bank. More luck came along in the shape of an angler wearing breast-high waders who stepped well out into the river and slid my landing net under it. By then a large crowd had gathered and in fear of the bailiff appearing I explained in a loud voice that it was amazing how a pike would pick up a single maggot intended for barbel. My careful explanation was not needed for as I began to remove the hooks with long-nosed pliers the still-active pike, which had not been fully played out, kicked hard and in full view of the audience disgorged my roach with the treble still firmly attached. The crowd were silent for a moment, then they started to mutter, and my popularity waned fast. The fish – a hen – weighed 6·3kg (14lb).

Pike fishing on the tideways is not always a happy-go-lucky sport. It has problems of its own which can be more frustrating than any encountered higher up the river in the freshwater reaches. One of those problems brings to my mind the Hampshire Avon again, for during the pike fishing season and in early summer great rafts of cut weed float downstream not just early in the season but throughout the pike-fishing period as well. So bad is it that one suspects that it is raked from the water and piled high only to be kicked back in to be flushed downstream when the first winter floods come along. But throughout the country there is far too much rubbish in our rivers, more so in winter when the fishery lies below a town or village. An example of this is the upper end of a Welsh tideway where I spent long periods fishing for pike, but had to abandon my efforts for days at a time. Large pieces of wood, plastic bottles, trees, bankside vegetation of all kinds would pass on its way downstream only to be carried back on the next tide. Sadly, I remember giving up after seeing the same dead and bloated sheep, its legs in the air, travelling back and forth for four days. The last thing I wanted to do was hook the distended stomach of that frightful thing.

Welsh tideways are quite different from others and they are often a total waste of time to fish. The principal problem is that of colour when the slightest of rainfalls can stain the water a rich cocoa-brown that smothers all angling activities because the bait is simply not visible. This thick water also leads to mud and silt being deposited in huge banks that prevent live- or deadbaiting close to the bottom even when the flood has subsided. Spinning is still effective, though, and my preference is for that style whenever I am fishing upper tidal water in the Principality – but beware!

One day while standing alone day-dreaming and casting a spinner on a winter's day I was suddenly surrounded by dozens of bodies, including serious-faced policemen, and felled to the ground. It took a lot of explaining by me before the Water Authority bailiffs and local police could appreciate that the mad Englishman would actually fish for the coarse species and that I was not spinning out of season for 'real' fish such as salmon or sewin.

There are many fishermen who have the idea that winter pike fishing on the tideways benefits from a rise in water temperature as the tide makes, this warmer water staying until the tide drops and leaves low, cold water. This fluctuation is supposed to induce fish to feed, but it is a fallacy. Over a period of 16 outings in one season I kept a record of the water temperature before high tide, at the peak of the tide and at the ebb. It showed that there was no upward temperature movement of any kind. But it did show a *drop* in temperature on two occasions, both of them when snow broth got into the river following a rapid upstream thaw. A cold stream was held back by the rising tide and then further cooled by a biting east wind driving across the wide river.

If there is an all-important advantage to any angler in tidal fishing it must come from the increased activity forced on fish as the water rises. Currents change and eddies form, dried-out areas become flooded; these cause fish to move about, use up energy and as a result start searching for food, some of which may be stirred up by the tidal movement itself. Pike, in common with all the species present, will be thus affected and will react to the presence of food. My own pleasure (and in view of the incident in Wales I have described above I should add 'only where and when it is legal') is to spin or plug-fish, both styles suiting the majority of waters and on bigger rivers at least enabling a far larger area to be searched than by the use of live or deadbait. Of course, if one has a boat, that ultimate luxury allows the angler to cover any water thoroughly.

In tidal waters large spinning baits are quite unnecessary, for I have repeatedly tried large spoons, leaf spinners or wobblers where there has been sufficient depth to justify their use and to allow their correct working, but I have never achieved that pattern of consistent success which is what the angler should seek to attain. One might take a fish here and there with a large lure, but more and certainly equally good fish have fallen to a small Mepps or Toby regardless of the depth and acreage of the water being fished.

But for all their effectiveness, using small spinners on large waters leaves much to be desired. One searches the edges and obvious lies within easy casting distance but sooner or later you are going to need some weight to achieve longer casting. I detest having any weight on my spinning outfits because of the 'keyhole' factor, when the weight travels faster than the spinner so that it becomes caught round the trace. Theoretically it can be solved by moving the lead farther back but in practice it still happens, often without apparent cause. Worse still is the attraction that lead seems to hold for pike, especially on tideways. These fish will often lunge at the weight and then turn away totally ignoring the spinner with its hooks. I once tried fitting a single treble to a lead and thought that I had found the answer but it turned out to be yet another loser. One has to face the fact that if weight is needed for attaining the required casting distance not only must it be enough for efficient casting, it must be designed for the job. There is a way of avoiding some of the false strikes which one gets on weights; it is by painting the leads a light blue instead of leaving them in their traditional dark green finish. It will not cut out all those false strikes, but you will find enough improvement to make to the tedious task worth your while.

Plug sizes are of less importance than their construction and the angler who fails to read the water and selects a deep diver at the wrong state of the tide soon pays expensively for his mistake. One only needs to take a few spinners in the tackle box, most of them spares in case of loss, but it is essential to have an adequate range of plugs if the water is to be properly covered during the various states of the tide. It has already been stressed elsewhere in this book, but, again, I would repeat that your plugs must earn their place in the box by their performance in the water. The kinds that do show a good return are the various floating/diving models, and the differently shaped deep divers, those with a big metal lip that can pull the body beneath a tidal swell in seconds. For freshwater plug fishing, the colour I prefer is yellow, either in whole or part, whereas on tidal stretches I have no doubt that silver is by far the most effective colour and a good bright silver too, reminiscent of dace, bleak or roach moving quickly in the current. All this means you must convert your plugs into new colorations but the effort will be rewarded.

Is tidal fishing worth while? This depends on the waters of that nature which are available to you and also on how much you enjoy your sport. If you only consider pike fishing in terms of weight caught then forget tidal fishing. It is not the kind of water where you will regularly find double-figure fish, although I am sure that I know of at least two waters where pike of 13·6kg (30lb) could be possible. Unfortunately the vastness of them would make the man-hours necessary to find the pike far too many to be a worth-while exercise. But if one enjoys pike fishing just for what it is, a challenge strictly related to the number of fish in the water one is fishing, then the search for them is something I am prepared to undertake. The hours I have spent pike fishing must run into hundreds if not thousands and over the years I have landed many grand fish. On the other hand, much of that time has been spent through force of circumstance and not from first choice.

When really hard weather strikes, and still-waters become sheeted with ice, with more encrusting the banks to make line cutting and fraying a probability, the tideways will still be open and their daily flow for all intents and purposes unaffected. They will also offer fair sport on occasion in spite of the temperature dropping below freezing. This does not mean that pike can be caught from the tideway when iceflows are drifting down thick and fast, but they are places where fish can be caught when there is just no chance elsewhere. If there is one basic lesson to be learned about pike fishing it is that one must know where the fish are.

8
The Future

How often have I heard it said that one should never look back in time! Surely, the past is finished and of no consequence, while the future must be everything. But history is recorded so that we may learn both of the people and the exploits of the past, to profit by the mistakes of others and to benefit from Man's discoveries, those rare moments of glory. These things hold good through angling, and perhaps it is no coincidence that those whose writing is concerned with angling history usually do so remembering only the good, their words couched in prose dripping with nostalgia, recalling palmy days when the fish gave themselves up by the cartload and anglers were gentlemen all who not only played a straight bat but also fished a clean, tight line.

With 50 years of angling behind me practically all devoted entirely to pike fishing I have decidedly mixed views not only on that which is now history, but also on many present-day practices including current opinions, some sound, some hysterical, that are freely voiced and written. Perhaps I can best explain my views by comparing the angler of the thirties as I remember him and how he went about his sport, with the angler of the eighties, taking care to acknowledge not only that which was and still is good, but also that which could be construed as bad.

Even allowing for a class system that was probably second to none in the civilised world, the pike angler of the thirties was regarded by one and all on the fishing scene as a very coarse fellow. He was lampooned frequently in cartoons, often being depicted with a large bottle of beer, plus a red, runny nose and dressed in an assortment of clothing that would do a rag-and-bone merchant proud. Of course, this image was not without some truth, but with an economic depression even deeper than today's few people had money to spare for winter clothing specifically designed for fishing.

Pike anglers were mostly solitary figures then: occasionally one might come across a couple fishing together, but generally it would be one man on his own and his age would be in the early twenties. My memory is that this was the age when one was qualified to go and fish for what was always referred to in the coarse angling Press as the 'Freshwater shark', below that age one was expected to conform to fishing for roach, dace and chub with perhaps an occasional tench. Carp – big carp – were nothing but legends for the most part.

In retrospect one obviously had to be of mature age and healthy disposition to be a pikeman. The only mode of transport was train or bus, always leaving a long walk either to the water or along the bank and more often than not one's finances dictated that that transport be ignored, so it would be a long footslog or pushbike ride to reach the waterside. The result was that only a short day could be spent actually fishing.

Not only finance but physique too played its part in making the pikeman's patch a very parochial one. The combined weight of wooden rods with their solid brass fittings, large wooden Nottingham-style reels (usually turned from walnut), wooden shafted and iron-rimmed landing nets, a hefty metal gaff without which one could not really be called a pike angler – all that plus terminal tackle, sandwiches and a thermos would be carried in a large wooden box that also served as a seat and which needed a fair amount of brawn to carry and which probably also helped to foster the 'coarse fellow' image.

What were the rewards in those years that are now past? Never tremendous. Of course, there were the privileged few in the upper classes who were able to fish select waters where massive bags of fish were caught, but the average angler was content to talk of 'a fish' and if it was big, then so much to the good. There was none of today's obsession with big catches, record-breaking weights, massive lists of double-figure fish: what came along was enough and more often than not that fish, regardless of size, was removed from the water either to be eaten (the usual fate in country areas) or to be taken home and displayed as a tribute to the angler's skill and daring. And within 24 hours the carcass was thrown into the dustbin. Very few, very special fish actually reached the magic portals of a glass case.

How different it all was when compared with today's pike fishing scene! Now, distance is no barrier, in fact the prospect of travelling to deserted, unexplored places is a positive spur. There is no difficulty in carrying tackle, which in terms of payload has been reduced to at least half of that carried in the past. The tackle, too, is sophisticated beyond all belief when compared with that used even ten years ago, let alone 50 years.

You will note that I did not start this chapter by commenting on the image of the present-day pike angler. There is little need to, in fact, largely because that image has hardly altered. He is still regarded by many as the coarse man of angling. It is a sweeping generalisation in many cases, but a truism nevertheless which is perpetuated by a mindless few, fed for some reason by the progress in tackle and tactics that has developed in recent years and a strange spirit of competitiveness bordering on mania that has crept into the sport.

The need to boast of the numbers of fish that have been caught in their weight and size brackets – tens, twenties, thirties, and so on – seems to have spurred an all-out offensive by anglers on the majority of pike waters that can do little good either to the fish or to the image of the sport. To reach targets one can find men using half-a-dozen or more rods at a time, men who will camp out and live for several days at a time in a particular area or hotspot that is known to fish well, or hold fish of exceptional weight, and men who are so intent on playing the numbers game that without hesitation they will poach on other anglers' private fisheries, or on waters where fishing is not allowed at any time. They will then boast of the catch after carefully 'moving' the place of capture by hundreds of metres or yards, even more.

The result of all this is trampled banks that are a quagmire, rubbish by the cartload, irate landowners, and badly hooked fish – this especially so where a number of rods are used, some of which are often positioned out of the angler's immediate view; or, where a bite indicator has been fixed, out of his hearing. Worse still is the dropped-bait syndrome that is affecting so many day-fisheries where the pike have been so persecuted that they mouth, then instinctively drop any bait immediately when even the slightest resistance is felt. Then there is the discord with other anglers, especially the game fishermen who resent a mindless few who have through livebaiting tactics introduced coarse fish into trout waters.

24 *Modern-day angling has long gone electronic. These bite detectors have buzzers so that the angler is alerted when he has a take and does not have to spend all his time concentrating on the movements of his floats. The author, however, prefers the old-fashioned ways!*

All this will be denied, disbelieved or excused by the majority of pike anglers. The usual excuse is that only a very small minority are guilty of these practices, but my observations show a different picture. True, a very few may be responsible for one of these anti-social practices – but a few more will indulge in another, and so on, until at the end of the day, when all are added together, the few become a sizeable total.

What is the answer to these problems? First and foremost, the pike angler needs to do a massive restructuring job on his image. Though the anti-blood sports brigade are just waiting to seize any opportunity to strike at the cruelty aspect of livebaiting I am not convinced that abandoning the practice will affect the pikeman's image a great deal. The move would be interpreted as a sign of weakness and it would be followed by a fresh attack on some other point.

But our house should be put in order in every respect and there must be someone with sufficient inventiveness to design a rig for live fish that does not involve hooks being thrust into their bodies. Difficulties many anglers experience in removing hooks from pike are all too frequently seen (and focussed on by TV cameras to a point where the object of the film is lost) which can only bring bad publicity to the sport. But clubs of all kinds, not only those devoted to pike fishing, must endeavour by teach-ins to educate anglers on the right way to release a pike. More can and must be done along these lines and I do not exclude Water Authorities from taking action in this direction. These bodies have the resources and better means of using the media for publicity than many of the small clubs who try hard to improve the image of angling.

What other ways are there to improve this image? Well, the pike itself could certainly do with some elevation. If one takes a detailed look at the game and the sea fisherman you cannot fail to see that they are far more accepted by the public – both pro and anti-angling lobbies – than the pikeman. Why? It is because you hear time and time again that those anglers eat what they catch and somehow people see this as a matter of sense. In fact, while catching fish to put them back is not only regarded as an act of conservation by some, it is considered an act of stupidity by others. But if pike were bred, caught and then the best removed and eaten, much in the same way as the trout, I am sure that we would soon find ourselves with a totally different image both within and without the world of angling.

Certainly, eating would be a large improvement on the gradually disappearing habit of mounting big fish, which would in many cases

25 *This 15kg (33lb 12oz) pike was taken from the River Thurne by the late Dennis Pye in the early sixties, who had it on the wall of his fish-and-chip shop. It then passed through the hands of three owners and was subject to restoration for five years before being acquired by its present owner, Vic Gibson*

have been better returned to the water. I have to admit, however, that to see a well-preserved fish is still a pleasure and I often look and wonder at the circumstances surrounding the capture of some of the older cased specimens.

The story behind the pike shown in Photograph 25 and held by Vic Gibson is very interesting. This fish was caught by the late Dennis Pye in the early sixties on the River Thurne, close to the entrance of Martham South Broad, on a roach livebait. Pencilled on the mounting board behind the fish is its weight – 15kg (33lb 12oz). For some years the fish hung, uncased, on the wall in the fish-and-chip shop that Dennis owned, and after the shop closed down, shortly before his death, Dennis presented the fish to a young angler and admirer. From there it passed to a second owner and eventually, badly in need of repair, the fish reached a taxidermist in Edmonton and work on restoration was carried out over a period of five years.

It was during this time that Vic managed to acquire the fish and he now has it at his home. It still needs a large sum of money to be spent not only on renovating the fins and body but on a case. I wonder how many other pike that have been preserved have seen such a long period between capture and final home? Or have had so much money spent on them!

There has got to be a drastic change in the pike angler's outlook on his fish from that held today. To take and destroy a pike – even by eating it, let alone by mounting it – is regarded with shouts of shame and horror. One might almost imagine that a crucifixion was taking place so loud and prolonged are the wails of distress. But like it or not a pike is merely a fish just the same as any other on the fishmonger's slab, and incidentally it is a valuable food source. If you do not believe me then eat the next small jack you catch. And for the record, pike are frequently seen on menus on the Continent, so what we did not eat might well be exported.

I feel that a slow change along some of the lines that I have described is taking place. Today, many of the owners of reservoirs for trout fishing are using pike anglers in an attempt to curb their excessive pike population – every fish in a trout reservoir other than the trout itself seems to be excessive! I have watched with interest the culling at my nearest reservoir, Bewl Bridge, since its opening in 1982, and both disturbing and interesting results are beginning to emerge.

In the three years from 1982 to 1984, 627 pike up to 4·5kg (10lb) were caught, while 56 were taken in the 4·5–9kg (10–20lb) range and ten weighing over 9kg (20lb). These are merely figures, an indication of the pike in the water, or perhaps an indication of the assistance given by pikemen to the trout angler. But a closer examination of these figures reveals a systematic shift in the pike population as the result of pike culls. The numbers of fish up to 4·5kg (10lb) taken in 1982 was 155; in 1983, 235 and in 1984, 237. In other words, in spite of bulk removal there was an increase in the numbers of small fish.

Now consider the pike in the 4·5–9kg (10–20lb) range. In 1982, 42 were landed, 8 in 1983 and 6 in 1984. So there was a decline in bigger fish and this continues into the numbers of fish over 9kg (20lb). Here the figures were 7 in 1982, 2 in 1983 and 1 in 1984. Again a decrease in numbers, all of which must be to the good – or so the trout angler would probably say. But that assumption is completely wrong. As every pikeman knows big pike eat little pike and the decline in big fish at Bewl Bridge has sparked off a population explosion of smaller fish in the water, and that must do little to preserve fish over 4·5kg (10lb) which can reduce the vast numbers of smaller fish chomping their way through trout. And better, there would be an increase of sport for the pike angler, a factor we shall examine later.

More importantly, there would be no need to cull every year. By natural selection the pike population would control itself. You see, the problem of culling is that often nobody wants the fish that are removed. The year 1985 was such a case at Bewl Bridge, where it was known that those fish caught would probably find no waters to which they could be transferred. It was this situation, I feel sure, that resulted in the rather stupid and very damaging action of the angler shown in the colour photograph on page 00. What is accepted on today's fishery becomes tomorrow's habit and problem.

One reservoir has made a significant step forward in elevating pike fishing to manageable, integrated and sensible proportions. At Ardingly, the owner has combined pike and trout fishing on equal terms, with both sections available on a day or season ticket basis.

26 *The author calls this 'armchair fishing'. It is the set-up facing anglers at Bewl Bridge, Kent. On pike-cull days the boats are allocated in advance, the anglers receive a briefing from the Head Bailiff so that the water is properly covered to remove as many pike as possible and also to ensure that a good day's sport is enjoyed by all*

27 *A 'Le Mans' start to a pike cull in morning mist and sun at Bewl Bridge. There is no competition for the prime hotspots; each angler knows where he is going to fish before he sets out*

There is, in fact, an overlap of seasons during October when both trout anglers and pikemen ply their sport without rancour on either side.

There, the pikeman can fish with up to three rods, a sensible number that can be controlled, and to ensure that unwanted fish are not introduced only coarse fish caught at the reservoir may be used as livebaits. Boats may be hired; in fact, everything is available to help the angler, but with one important difference. In this reservoir the pike are returned, and pike *do* run big with few really small specimens being taken.

Here, I feel sure, is the future of pike angling in this country with managements acknowledging that the pike is a fish high on the angler's quarry list, taking care to produce a healthy return in terms of sport and finance for an outlay of very little labour. Though there will be some who will scoff at my conjecture that one day we shall see pike farmed and fished for on equal terms with trout, I have a feeling that I will be proved right. If you do not believe me, then study trawling practices round our coast and the steady decline in the numbers of fish that are being landed. Then think of the fickle fancies of the eating public and realise that before the days of the package holiday both squid and octopus were unknown foods in British restaurants. Shortage of other fish, and the chance to experiment with new foods could well put the pike on the commercial map.

But before much of this can happen we shall have to conquer the looming hazard of sport sharing. Today, pressure is heavy on every scrap of water in the country not only by anglers but by wind-surfers, water skiers, yachtsmen, scuba divers, ornithologists and so on. And as each and every one of them requires something different in the way of water environment some stormy days are ahead.

The yachtsman, for instance, and the windsurfer require open waters where there is nothing in the way of background trees or woodland to block the wind. Those who water-ski want trees removed from around the bankside, while the ornithologist demands that everything be left as it is, so that wildlife 'may benefit', whatever that means. What the ultimate solution to these diverse demands may be cannot be imagined at the moment. Where the waters are big, then everyone co-exists without too much aggravation, but pressure on waters for sporting purposes, especially in the south of England, is enormous and some pretty drastic rethinking, rescheduling and reorganising must take place if we are not to do irreparable damage to that which we have at the moment.

We shall survive one way or another, no doubt, and with resolution on the part of the pikeman there must be an improvement in attitude and sport. Certainly we have moved a long way since Izzak Walton preached 'To be quiet, and go a-angling'.

Bibliography

Bickerdyke, John. *Angling for Pike*, 19th Edn (Thorsons Publishers, 1959)

Buller, Fred. *Pike* (Macdonald, 1971)

Buller, Fred. *The Domesday Book of Mammoth Pike* (Stanley Paul, 1979)

Chillingworth, William. *Tactics for Big Pike* (Beekay Publishers, 1959)

Fickling, Neville. *Pike Fishing in the 80s* (A. & C. Black, 1982)

Gammon, Clive. *Hook, Line and Spinner* (Heinemann, 1959)

Gay, Martin. *Beginner's Guide to Pike Fishing* (Pelham Books, 1975)

Gibbinson, Jim. *Pike* (Osprey, 1974)

Jardine, Alfred. *Pike and Perch* (Lawrence & Bullen, 1898)

Keal, William. *Bill Keal's Book of Fishing* (Clipper Press, 1972)

Marshall-Hardy, Eric. *Angling Ways*, 10th Edn, revised by Len Cacutt (Barrie & Jenkins, 1973)

Maunsell, George William. *Fisherman's Vade Mecum* (Philip Allan, 1933)

Rickards, Barrie. *Big Pike* (A. & C. Black, 1986)

Rickards, Barrie, and Whitehead, Ken. *Spinners, Spoons and Wobbled Baits* (A. & C. Black, 1977)

Rickards, Barrie, and Gay, Martin. *Pike Angler's Manual* (A. &. C. Black, 1987)

Rickards, Barrie, *Pike, Step-by-Step* (Cassell, 1976)

Spencer, Sidney. *Pike on the Plug* (H. F. & G. Witherby, 1936)

Wanless, Alexander. *The Science of Spinning for Salmon and Trout* (Herbert Jenkins, c1947)

Index